Praise for *The Green Funeral*

"When it comes to funerals in the Black community, the common questions are 'who has the body?' and 'what cemetery is your loved one's final resting place?' but the question we are not asking is: how can we honor God, our loved one and the land with an ethical, toxin-free, green funeral and natural burial? In *The Green Funeral*, Sequola Dawson writes with pastoral care, a detailed eye to Black traditions, and a theological framework that invites the Black Church, the funeral industry and the community into the conversation of 'going green.' We don't talk enough about deathcare, and how traditional 'preparing the body' practices can be toxic, causing us and the land to be exposed to harmful chemicals . . . but now we can with this well-researched book that offers the Black community a new aesthetic for discussing death, funerals and burials through an ecological lens that promotes care for all of God's creation."

—**Rev. Yvette R. Blair-Lavallais**, Ecowomanist and Adjunct Professor of Theologies of Land and Food, Memphis Theological Seminary

"Sequola Dawson provides a compelling theological account for thinking about faithful discipleship that encompasses an important, but too-often overlooked, aspect of Christian worship—our funeral practices. While rooted in the African

American tradition, this is a must read for all Christians who seek to honor God's covenant with integrity through our living and our dying."

—**Sarah Musser**, Consulting Faculty at
Duke Divinity School

"In *The Green Funeral: Honoring the Environment While Beautifying Funeral Practices*, Rev. Sequola Dawson speaks to the Black Church, but invites us all to contemplate our last impact on God's good earth. Let us all prayerfully consider returning to the dust from which we came as nourishment to the sacred land."

—**Rev. Carol L. Devine**, Director of Blessed Tomorrow

The Green Funeral

The Green Funeral

HONORING THE ENVIRONMENT WHILE BEAUTIFYING FUNERAL PRACTICES

SEQUOLA DAWSON

Foreword by
DR. DAVID EMMANUEL GOATLEY

Afterword by
DR. JONATHAN C. AUGUSTINE

Broadleaf Books
Minneapolis

THE GREEN FUNERAL
Honoring the Environment While Beautifying Funeral Practices

30 29 28 27 26 25 1 2 3 4 5 6 7 8 9

Library of Congress Control Number: 2025009678 (print)

Cover image: © 2025 Adobe Stock; 444240891 Abstract art gold tropical leaves background vector by Twins Design Studio
Cover design: Studio Gearbox

Print ISBN: 979-8-8898-3497-7
eBook ISBN: 979-8-8898-3498-4

CONTENTS

FOREWORD

FUNERALS ARE IMPORTANT in Christian communities. These services of worshiping God and remembering those who have died are opportunities to engage, seriously, the intersections of divinity and humanity. They bring together the eternal and the temporal in critical ways that seek to bring together both Christian hope and comfort for those who experience the physical loss of those with whom we have (or should have) loved. This is desperately and especially needed for believers around the world.

It seems that most people who have been socialized in or by the West struggle with the concept and the reality of death. There is a cultural preoccupation with defying rather than embracing aging. Many seem to desire to be eternally young and, thereby, forestall or ignore death. An industry flourishes with aids to help people appear more youthful than they really are. It helps to mask the appearance of the actual changes that are happening in our bodies across the years. We may pull one over on others, but unless we are seriously delusional, we who are aging are not fooling ourselves even while we may be trying to ignore realities. Even when death inevitably catches up with us, there is another industry—the funeral industry—that is particularly good at preparing a corpse to appear to be asleep. It is not uncommon to hear observers of a body prepared for a funeral comment on how good the dead body looks. Makeup and hair styling can work wonders—even for the dead.

Many cultures, however, value the aged. No sensible people assume that wisdom automatically accompanies the accumulation of years. I was once in a West African context when a situation turned volatile with the possibility of violence. A recognized older person soon arrived at the scene. One of the excited young adults began speaking assertively, and apparently angrily, as the elder inquired about the dispute. While I could not understand all the words pouring from the young man's mouth, I did recognize the words addressing the elder as, "Old man! . . . Old man!" I was certain that the situation was about to deteriorate. Fortunately, the "Old man" was able to deescalate the situation, and we were able to proceed safely. The elder later explained that the term "Old man" in that culture was equivalent (at least in the 1980s when this occurred) to someone in our context respectfully saying, "Sir."

Some cultures hold aging in higher esteem than others. Wisdom is part of responsible aging, and human viewpoint aligns more closely with divine outlook as disciples of Jesus grow closer and older and witness the hand of God and the embrace of the Spirit as the years go by. And part of the wisdom of aging is to see death not as something to avoid, but a reality to engage. It is coming, so it makes sense to accept and, ideally, embrace it as the door that leads from time to eternity.

Funerals follow death for followers of Christ. Sometimes funerals are beautiful expressions of affection for those of blessed memory and appreciation for how their lives have been instruments of God's love in the world. Reflections of experiences, conversations, and impact in the lives of others can help you to comfort in a time of loss. Seeing the difference that loved ones have made in peoples' lives and reminding each other of the victory of Christ Jesus over death helps believers to grieve with hope.

Regrettably, however, some funerals are filled with sorrow and hopelessness. Broken relationships, injurious words, angry feelings, painful memories, and the like are sometimes on full display at funerals. Unfortunately, some funerals become flashpoints of anger, betrayal, and emptiness rather than opportunities for worship, thanksgiving, loving recollections, and healing.

Sequola Dawson's experience as a minister to bereaved families has brought her into close proximity to families in their walk through death and decisions related to it. While ministering to the dying and those who love them, she has repeatedly witnessed decisions about what to do that are problematic emotionally, economically, environmentally, and ecclesiastically. Her education and experience in environmental sciences and Christian ministry position her better than most to understand the consequences of traditional decisions about funerals and to present an alternative that offers personal and familial healing, mitigates financial strain, leaves a light ecological footprint, and challenges churches to expand their priestly and prophetic imagination. While she offers particular attention to, and critique of, predominantly Black churches, her focus on the Black Church is a gift to the whole church.

Embracing *The Green Funeral* cuts against the grain of what many Western Christians have been taught to appreciate. Her text is an invitation to a deeper discipleship. She calls Christians and churches to turn away from guilt- or ego-driven funeral productions; unnecessary and unwise expenses and indebtedness; toxic decisions with devastating environmental impacts; and ecclesial complicity in practices that are harmful to families and the earth. This, in a sense, is a call to repent and be saved.

Dr. David Emmanuel Goatley
President, Fuller Theological Seminary
Pasadena, California
July 2024

1

Greening Death

AT DEATH, AMERICANS frequently seek to distance themselves from the natural process of decomposition. With little thought of what is going into the soil, we pollute the land and therefore harm the very thing that God loves and gives to us for our flourishing. The land supports and feeds us, and we are called to be in a covenantal relationship with it; yet so often we are not. For example, we bury our dead full of chemicals, unnecessarily embalming the bodies of our loved ones, and we place them in manufactured products, caskets also chemically treated. Certainly, we must consider the laws and legislation governing funeral practices. But might there be a larger story that is missed when we consider death and our relationship to the land? Despite the well-known Scripture, "you are dust, and to dust you shall return" (Gen 3:19), Christians fail to embrace the fullness of natural burials as we return to the land.

As a chaplain, director of bereavement, and minister of the Gospel, I focus on the Black Church's relative silence and its insufficient attention given to how our practices around death go against the foundational principle of covenant relationship and therefore distort our perceptions of Christian beauty. The green funeral engages aesthetics and ecological commitments, in and outside of the church, that will lead to the introduction of practices and of ministry that honor God and contribute to the care and sustainability of the earth.

I seek to make my case by leaning heavily on Leviticus to identify covenantal relationships and through obedience, help strengthen Black Church covenantal loyalty. Leviticus 26:42 says, "then I will remember my covenant with Jacob; I will remember my covenant with Isaac, and also my covenant with Abraham, and I will remember the land." I iterate the blessings for creation—land and people with rain, harvests, and fertility. With obedience to God's statutes and laws, Leviticus 26 says "I will grant peace in the land, and you shall lie down untroubled by anyone." (Lev 26:6; Everett Fox's translation). I use Leviticus 26:19–20 to suggest what disobedience would resemble and how the Black Church might sow its seed in vain. I translate disobedient practices such as burying money in fancy coffins, injecting dead bodies with toxic chemicals, and emitting harmful pollutants into the air with cremations. All these poisonous burial practices make "earth like copper" and infertile lands (Lev 26:19). But Leviticus teaches not to defile but to be clean and holy "for I the Lord your God am holy" (19:2).

I offer two lenses through which to examine the Church's care of creation: covenantal relationship and beauty. Through these lenses, I wish to see how covenantal commitments and aesthetic concerns hold up when they are placed into conversation with creation theology, environmentalism, and the current practices of the funeral industry, and how these values end up distorted by harmful church practices that do not honor creation. I hope to help the Church see differently, especially as concern for covenantal relationships and recognizing and celebrating the beauty of the world are already important to the church. As we return to dust, church congregants can be educated about and directed toward funeral options that uplift the foundational principle of covenantal relationship that has the potential to guide us toward caring, ecological practices. As committed Christian leaders, we must become more aware of how we attend to our dead and return them to the ground in the most life-giving of ways.

As an earth theologian, my mission is to create space to exercise love for God and love for God's creation, even in death. I hope to give rise to space to best cultivate and recultivate, call and recall, think and rethink, condition and recondition, engineer and reengineer, imagine and reimagine our interdependence with the land. Love for God and care for God's creation is the goal of *The Green Funeral.* There was a time when, as the assistant to the director of bereavement, I asked myself, Why am I called to go to so many funerals? Later, I understood that God was developing me as an earth theologian—one who pays attention to practices and processes of funerals. Since God said in Leviticus 26, "I shall remember the land," it is proper for us to remember the land, literally and figuratively, in our practices and processing as well. Lastly, it is my desire to aid families in having death conversations. I hope that my funeral rights will help my daughter and other family members to best process procedures inside of a death season; even if that is just knowing that I spoke of it often. I think this topic will resonate with other families.

In essence, my research investigates the incorporation of green burial practices into the Black Church funeral.

My goal is to explore how changing aesthetics among funeral practices in the Black Church might enable more faithful stewardship of God's creation in order to provide a blueprint for churches' bereavement practices that better witness to our commitment to our covenant with God in terms of how we use the gifts of creation God has so graciously given. A problem for the Black Church is tradition, culture, and a lack of education about green or natural burials. This book, however, is not meant to antagonize the rich and vibrant Black community but is a call to unity of the majority owners, the ones who own the frontiers, prairies, and pastures of America. For all of us to come together, realizing the past and to best step into the future as one. We are better together even in death. We are the land that we have fought for and have taken claim to. Yet it all belongs to God. Each person desires to live in dignity; and because I have worked much with grieving families I understand that each family desires to lay down in dignity. One of the more progressive options is through funeral and burial practice; through the thinking and rethinking of the land as God's and the relinquishing of it for all to have greater access. Currently the number of cemeteries and funeral homes per state that advertise a "no embalming" option are few. According to the Green Burial Council (GBC) website, Ohio has six, the most certified green burial cemeteries of any state in the United States (although other non-GBC certified cemeteries exist, they have not been certified by the GBC, the council that currently oversees this effort).

Although I come to this project as a Black Church member and with my own experience, my approach is informed by, and weighs heavily on, historical work and current literature. I will build upon that work and enter conversation with theologians and those in the funeral industry and the green burial fields to support the Black Church and others seeking to change how they interact with our planet.

The deathcare industry is dominated by tradition. With the current turn to natural burials, morticians must assess and reassess what green means from an economic perspective to their bottom line. Then as a value-add in the community, educate and promote green options. First, keeping a focus on land. The availability of land and resources are crucial to accessibility and reliability of green alternatives.

In these efforts, I give insight into the complexity of the African American relationship with the environment. I highlight the Black environmentalism work of Mark Stoll and Dianne Glave in *To Love of the Wind and the Rain*, a groundbreaking book that explores the relationship between African Americans and the environment and is an invaluable foundation for *The Green Funeral.* Glave and Stoll focus on rural African American women's experience to show that, despite the stereotype of not being interested in nature, they are rooted in the earth and outdoors.

James Cone, the founder of Black Liberation Theology, says that Black folk simply need to be brought to the environmentalism table and not left out. Cone argues that Black people *are* environmentalists; and Black folk have always had something to say about this topic. For *The Green Funeral,* Cone's opinion is important because it helps support and boost the interest of the Black community in the environment because environmental affairs are our, Black folk, affairs.

For a new generation, I introduce and present to others Bishop Ambrose of Milan (c. 339–397). Bishop Ambrose offers us what I call the true nature of beauty. He keeps the eyes forever focused on the glory of God and away from the trends that catch our daily attention. This view is critical as I seek to strengthen not only our inextricable tie with the land but, through the green funeral, our covenantal relationship with God.

Theologian Ellen Davis, my Duke Divinity School professor, in *Getting Involved with God* gives the green funeral, a delicate yet challenging perspective on God's creation. From Professor Davis, I first heard the concept of "the wearing of each other" where we are so tied not only to each other but to the land. Just as we put on or wear clothes, we carry each other's burdens and cares. We are to put on each other to include the land so that when this life is over, we simply lie down in one another. Professor Davis asserts that God is in covenant with Godself, the people, and the land. And therefore, we should be as well.

Likewise, Theologian Wille Jennings and Professor Norman Wirzba help us to strengthen our ecological faith with what I refer to as the soul and the soil. Jennings inextricably ties race and place as two sides of the same coin. First, Jennings gets to the heart of the matter (the soul) acknowledging that we, the people, are *possessed* by God, our Creator. We own nothing. Jennings makes the case for changing how we see ourselves and how we view land as dirt to gain the best chance for people to unite, to become one.

Professor Wirzba, in *Thanks for The Dirt*, writes that we increase our ecological faith with our connection to the soil. Wirba looks at the complex networking of the soil and of people toward the working of our interdependence. Wirzba asserts that with a spirit of gratitude for the soil, we should gain a basis for environmental ethics.

Dr. Betty Holley, my professor at Payne Theological Seminary, challenges the Black Church to think and rethink, to consider and reconsider strengthening our sustainability efforts. In an age of climate change, the Black Church is poised to do even greater things in environmentalism, a new aesthetic rooted in earth (land) and in covenant with God.

Candi Cann graces us with the history of funerals in America while Karla Holloway gives us the African American funeral experience. This helps to forge the way for Lee Webster, a former Board Member of the Green Burial Council (GBC), to offer a professional green burial perspective, a new aesthetic for the Western American culture. Webster is one who has researched green burials and offers objective data to support her commitment in the advancement of "greening death" in America.

Likewise, Suzanne Kelly brings a comprehensive look into natural burials—no embalming, no man-made synthetics, no vaults—this is greening death, hence the green funeral. Kelly presents the history of greening death and how greening death is beneficial for us today. I extend the green burial concept formed by the GBC. Although the GBC in the green burial promotes no embalming, the concept of "funeral" remains general. For *The Green Funeral*, and for the Black Church and its community, the concept of funeral is key and aids in the preparation and allows for space and time to think green well before the thought of burial and cemetery. For Black folk the ritual of "funeral" and honoring our dead is still key. *The Green Funeral* does just that.

Then James Wilson offers a perspective on why greening death is important to a younger generation. Wilson recounts greening death conversations with his mother and grandmother and how those conversations have impacted his thinking toward the planning of his own death and conversations with his children about death.

Ultimately, the word of God places the seal on Black folk and the environment, in Genesis 2:7 when the Lord God formed man from the dust of the ground. Finally, in Leviticus 26:42 (KJV), God said, "Then I will remember my covenant with Jacob, and also my covenant with Isaac, and also my covenant with Abraham will I remember; and I will remember the land." *The Green Funeral* stands firm on the word of God and believes that God's word, God's promises are true. So there is no need to worry, even in death.

2

The Setting

AS A CHAPLAIN within the American health care system and now pastor, I have been called to the bedside of those who are *actively dying*. Generally, *actively dying* signifies the final stage of death where the patient is expected to die within a matter of hours or days, usually three days. The aesthetics of a cold hospital—the polar-express white walls, the hard white porcelain floors, the cold touch of the stethoscope, and the ice-cold temperature of the rooms—do not create the warmest of places to cuddle next to the dying or to display the soul pain that gushes uncontrollably from the gut. Yet, as a vibrant life grows dim and the determination of *actively dying* is made, the hospital pastoral care staff exhibits a high level of preparedness for death—enhanced communications, ensuring backup coverage is intact, and that all technological systems are working and engaged. Through the warmth of hospital staff, comfort care is offered: no more medicines to combat disease, just soothing medicines are administered; the lights are dimmed and peaceful music is played.

Likewise, as a minister of the Gospel within a Black Church, when death is *imminent*, the church leadership goes on high alert as internal communications are made and an abundance of prayers for the sick and for the family ensue. The warmth of the congregation heats up, as if the oak pews were on fire, baking cakes, frying chicken, and distributing other goods, all to ensure the family is comforted.

With death waiting in the wings, preparations need to be made. Upon receiving a notice of death or a request for funeral services, the church leadership is in high gear—meetings are scheduled with the family and discussions begin about the Order of Service, who will participate, and the costs (if any). Only in extreme cases, such as an expectation of a very large crowd, have I witnessed the church be proactive with the scheduling of a formal staff meeting before a funeral. In addition, it appears that only a few post-funeral evaluation meetings are held. All too often a funeral is pieced together inside of an existing standard Order of Service and, for the most part, the preparation is reactive rather than proactive by nature. Death care is not just for the dead but for the living. In times of death, the world may appear a blur and unreal. For many, the desire is to pinch oneself or to wake up and hope it all goes away. But the reality is that although one must go through the cloudy days, for those providing service, extreme care must be exhibited, both in the words expressed and the dollars spent. Often the grieving family has not preplanned or prepared, so while grieving they are obligated to simply "get through" discussions and make difficult decisions.

In such a reactionary state, the service provider rarely has room for extended discussions regarding lessons learned from funerals past, let alone extending the conversation toward considering environmental factors and other concerns. It is beneficial for all involved, beforehand, to take a closer look at the dynamics and details at play. For the church, being proactive means to remember and plan for the uniqueness of each family and to consider each family outside of the standard order of business, making space for creativity and uniqueness to shine. For the family, being proactive is to know your options, research the funeral home (if used) before time, ask questions, request an itemized cost sheet, and understand depository options. In other words, to prepare oneself to not be in a position, when everything is over, of saying, "I wish I would have done it differently." At the end of the day, all parties want to be able to say, "it is well with my soul."

In 2016, my church received news of the death of one of our members. Before the woman died, she spoke often to her children about having obtained life insurance and a burial plot (plots for the family) and wanting to being buried in all white—white clothing and a white casket. Every first Sunday, the mother sat with the other missionaries of the church all dressed in white. So, to be buried in white was an acknowledgment of the life that she lived—trusting in the Lord and working for the church. Because she was a member of a local church, the family respected and held the mother's church membership as sacred. Therefore, the family knew that this church was where the funeral services would be held. In addition, the family remembered their mother's wishes, taking her wishes into initial conversations with the funeral home directors (morticians); then again, into a separate meeting with the church. Because of some preplanning discussions (however small) and because of the way the mother lived a life that reflected both her Christian and cultural values, the family had a sense of peace because they were carrying out their mother's wishes. Thus, the family felt at ease, especially as the morticians were members of the same local church as the family (the mortician/owner sang beside the mother in the senior choir), and the funeral home was just down the street from the church, part of the community that the deceased had lived in and been cherished by.

However, although the deceased had given some thought to certain aspects of her funeral, there were gaps in her planning. When the family went to the funeral home, the funeral home attendant acknowledged their deceased mother had been picked up and was now in their care and was being prepared. Not wanting to know the specifics, the family did not ask what "being prepared" meant, but because of tradition and culture, it was understood that "being prepared" meant the mother was being embalmed—being preserved and being made ready for presentation. Understandably, these details, at that time, were too much for the family to consider in any depth. As the meeting began, the mortician presented the price list of services, which were itemized with no discussion regarding options. Since the family felt a closeness with the funeral home, they were willing to pay the listed price without negotiating. For example, when it came to selecting a casket, the family was moved to the casket room for selection, and for convenience and streamlining of services, the family decided to go with what the funeral home offered without deviation and not to create more stress. A family member did note that Costco was selling caskets, and the attendant confirmed that this was an option, but this was not pursued. In the end, the casket was purchased based on color, aesthetics—shiny, brass handles, and custom wording/stitching—and price. No formal preplanning with the funeral home had been done, so the family was there making decisions under the duress of the hour. The cremation option was never placed on the table; maybe because the mortician felt that she knew the family very well. For this family, the mortician was correct. They did not want to consider cremation.

Next, the conversation turned to vaults—whether a vault was needed or not, or a vault with liner. The family chose the vault that would keep water from seeping in. Fortunately, the mother had purchased burial plots many years before with the family in mind. Other family members were already laid to rest there. Toward the end of the meeting, the mortician "threw-in" an extra funeral car at no charge. The price for the embalming and casket remained at list price.

At the second (final) visit to the funeral home, the deceased was ready for family viewing. Standing at the casket, the mortician removed the light delicate covering from the mother's face and continued to fix every small detail. This well-known mortician was a friend of the mother. No doubt, this brought comfort to the family. The mother was freshly preserved and dressed in all white, as was the casket. The inner casket was lined with engraved material that read: "May the Lord watch between me and thee while we are absent one from another. Amen." Although difficult, these things brought the family comfort as they did what needed to be done, the way they thought it should be according to the traditions in their culture and church. "Your mother looks good," the mortician said. "Yes, she does," the family responded. The mortician said it was not hard to make the family's mother look lovely—"Your mother has always been a beautiful woman," the mortician noted.

The church, the funeral home, and the family all worked together to agree on a date and time for the funeral and to ensure it was conducted without a hitch. For years, the "viewing" of the deceased—where the community is invited to see (to view) the deceased body and to share in the grief—was done the evening before a funeral. However, by the new millennium, many viewings were being conducted on the same day as the funeral. This helped to spare the family repeated trips and avoided aggravated pain and anguish. This family chose for the viewing, funeral, and burial to occur all on the same day. Inside of a set viewing hour, the mother lay in state with an open casket. An hour later, the casket was closed, and the mother was funeralized.

After the church service, all attendees drove to the cemetery. The cemetery procession was routed on a busy highway. The grave diggers—appointed by the city or the cemetery staff—were there awaiting the arrival of the family. The vault was already in place in the grave. (If you could balance yourself well, you could look into the grave and get a glimpse of the vault.) Upon arrival, the pallbearers placed the casket above the grave and the services began. The family followed the directions of the church leaders and morticians. Upon the benediction, the family was directed to leave the cemetery while the casket was still above ground. Once all the funeral cars left the cemetery, the graveyard workers completed the burial process. The family was instructed to come back the next day, to view the covered grave.

A North Carolina Black Church Funeral Model

The relationship between North Carolina Black Churches and the North Carolina Black funeral industry is complex. In *The Glad Funeral*, I expound on how the Black Church helps the grieving family *carry the load of the casket*. To *carry the load of the casket* goes beyond walking the grief-stricken family through stages of grief but through funeral processing. But what else might *carrying the load of the casket* imply? To what extent can funeral practices breach the covenantal relationship with God, if at all?

African American funeral homes in North Carolina, like other African American funeral homes, grew out of the ugliness of segregation to become mainstays of the Black community and culture. In North Carolina, Black-owned and operated funeral homes, in association with the Funeral Directors and Morticians Associations (FDMA) of North Carolina, promote excellence in service to the grieving families of North Carolina. From central North Carolina—Perry-Brown, Hargett, Johnson and Sons; to the sandhills—Paye, Wiseman, Colvin, Dafford; to the mountains—Murrough, Wilkins-Hart, Morris; and to the coast—Peoples, Haywood, Shaw (just to name a few), all have sustained legacies rich in history and tradition. Notably, the prominent funeral home Scarborough and Hargett of Durham is a Black funeral home business in North Carolina with a long history. In 1871, grocer Joseph Crooms Hargett started a funeral home business in Kinston, North Carolina. In 1888, John Clarence Scarborough, Sr. joined the business and in 1906 became the first African American in North Carolina to be a licensed funeral director. In a 2015 article, fourth generation mortician John Clarence Scarborough, III tells the story of his great-grandfather joining the funeral business with Hargett to create dignity in death after a preeminent Black figure in Kinston died and "the white mortician held his viewing in the basement instead of the chapel and used a wagon instead of a horse-drawn hearse."

With this commitment shown toward the Black community, yet with minimal options or variations in the larger capitalization of North Carolina's funeral industry, I noticed patterns of funeral processing. Similar to some African funeral traditions, a North Carolina Black Church funeral is a communal event where, in the past, a wreath would be placed on the porch and neighbors would know death was present. Then the community cooks would bring food to the bereaved family. To the Black Church, funerals are like family reunions where people you have not seen in years come to pay respect, reconcile old wounds, and reflect on all the years that have gone by. Whether death is expected or comes quickly, when death comes, no family wants to be perceived as ill-prepared. This time is not only for grieving, but also for the family of the deceased to act as if they have everything together and not pieced-together at the last minute. Ultimately, during their final acts for the deceased, the family wants the world to know that their loved-one was loved. The Black Church helps the funeral come together beautifully, but invariably it moves on to the next family without discerning how to help the families to see better alternatives, including ecological friendly options, that might better honor God and thus their loved ones.

With such loyalty toward the Black community and with minimal options or variations in North Carolina's funeral industry, I noticed patterns of funeral processing across the state. Like Scarborough, I have noticed that "Black funeral practices tend to be more old-fashioned, where for instance, viewings have remained in favor." A public viewing of an embalmed body is a staple of the traditional funeral. Mortician and author Caitlin Doughty says that not only does the traditional funeral include "the public viewing of an embalmed body but a casket is communicative of social status, and a large stone marking one's grave" is also normative.

In addition, there exists a tightly coupled partnership with the Black Church and the local Black-owned funeral homes. This bond is so tightly woven that it is difficult to tell them apart, mainly because many funeral home employees also serve in some clergy functions or ecclesial roles in Black churches. Karla Holloway says that because "many Black funeral homes were themselves owned and operated by preachers [this] indicated the degree of intimacy the institutions shared." This intimacy created a juxtaposition of Black people being proud of Black-owned businesses and seeing our folk not only survive but also thrive in business, while at the same time, presenting an opportunity to be reluctant to challenge or push back on the practices of the local funeral homes that have been known, or widely rumored around town, to practice toxic, or at minimum, westernized capitalistic behaviors that damage the psyche of the Black community. From the extreme practice after the Civil War of "we'd just mix our own embalming chemicals—formaldehyde, alcohol, glycerin, borax, and water"—to what today can be considered, at best, as a *simply* wasteful practice of putting money in the ground, might there be ways in which the funeral industry practices are not aligned with strong Christian values that are rooted in a covenant relationship with God concerning care for creation? In North Carolina, the relationship between the Black Church and the Black funeral industry remains tightly coupled.

Born and reared in North Carolina where my parents were church leaders, I have attended more than my share of funerals. Like many, my family knew morticians personally because we were in the same church and community. My mother sang in the choir with the local mortician and I grew up with the daughter of the mortician. Yet, as funerals and rituals are important to the Black Church, the broader view of death care outside of the four walls of the church to include environmentalism has ground to gain.

The North Carolina Black Church funeral finds itself functioning in ways that align with other profit-making businesses in America. This can be seen by examining the North Carolina Funeral Directors Association's (NCFDA) four categories of service that comprise funeral costs. They include:

a. Funeral Director Services—a staff's professional services, facilities and equipment usage, and merchandise purchases: casket, vault, clothing;
b. Disposition Services—earth interment, the opening and closing of the grave, and cremation costs. The cost of the urn is separate.

c. Memorialization Options—for example, a monument or grave marker.
d. Miscellaneous Expenses—flowers, honorarium for the clergyman, newspaper notices, additional vehicles or out-of-town transportation of the body and other items, many of which involve the discretion of the family.

The North Carolina Funeral Directors Association reports average funeral costs of $6,000 to $9,500. Table 2.1 shows a representative break-down.

Virginia Beard and William Burger in *Change and Innovation in the Funeral Industry* describe early American death rituals as simple—"funerals were not lengthy events, the body was handled by the family with no embalming, and with

Table 2.1. The North Carolina Funeral Directors Association's Break-Down of Average Funeral Costs.

Expenses	Percentage
Merchandise (casket and interment receptacle)	30
Salaries	25
Facilities and Equipment	10
Cash advances for convenience of client	10
Profit	9
Administrative and General	6
Automotive	5

simple caskets." But this simplicity changed over time with the Industrial Revolution and "the increase in economic affluence to display wealth." By the end of the nineteenth century, displays of wealth and classism were in full view—the type of hearse, the number of volleys fired to honor the deceased, the number of death rings given to the mourners to remember the occasion, locations of internment, the make of the headstone, and even the length of the funeral, some "lasting 3 to 4 days." In North Carolina, such displays were also found.

Putting Money in the Ground

Holloway notes that there is an element of *display* in the Black funeral. For example, not only is the body of the deceased on display but wealth (or the pretense of wealth) is on display: the number of funeral cars, the color and finish of the casket—satin bronze or gold plated. Holloway recalls historical mortician practices often involved "the *swindling* mortician using a cheap coffin with a lot of paint." This contributes to the perception that "the negro will do a lot to be sure of a classy funeral." In a move to suggest an elite status, Black Republicans of the mid-1900s began turning from the Black-owned funeral homes to white funeral homes. However, this move has never been widely replicated except—ironically—in cases of pauper or welfare burials, Holloway explains.

Yet to some, not skimping on funerary displays is advantageous. La Trese Evette Adkins, in her dissertation, "And Who Has the Body," explores the historical significance of African American funeral displays. Adkins concludes that she cherishes not splurging on funerary display and that not skimping is a "cosmological investment in ancestors by pouring our hearts and pooling our resources into funerals." Such a desire to honor the dead is understandable, and to critique the celebration of our loved ones and the good intentions of the Black Church, the Black funeral industry, and the Black community at large that have experienced such oppression is not my intention here. We need to celebrate the lives of our friends and family—it is *how* we do so that is a concern.

With Noble Intentions

I recognize the noble intentions of families seeking to honor their loved ones and the reasons for the Black Church's funeral practices. With noble intentions "the ritual formality and spectacle of Black funerals and burials were [and are] clearly deliberate attempts to make the home-going ceremonies of African Americans underscore or encourage a view of each life as important" and of value. This is especially true when we live in an America that has repeatedly shown that the commitments, choices, thoughts, feelings, memories, and hopes of Black and Brown people are of little or no value. The failed oppressive capitalistic system in which America was founded aids in the systemic injustices of our bodies and communities, yielding emotional weights that are difficult to overcome, says activist Prentis Hemphill. Hemphill surmises that our current systems continue to traumatize Black people and ensure we have little time and energy to heal and few resources at hand. Thus, the Black funeral is seen as an opportunity to show reverence, respect, honor, and dignity, even while the services that create the funeral are subject to the same capitalist imperatives that are frequently oppressive.

The morticians attempt their best to beautify the deceased given the circumstances. Embalming is not only a vocation, but an art—the art of prolonging the semblance of life—says a North Carolina mortician and long-time embalmer. During a period of his own family bereavement due to the death of a cousin, he shares, "I cannot make her beautiful because I am so accustomed to seeing her alive"—as if to say that his best effort to hold death at bay is not good enough. I attended that funeral, and the deceased looked very pleasant, peaceful, and as the old folks would say, "she looked good," "she looked like herself," and "she looked like she was asleep."

The Black funeral often gives space for one to be fully human, emotional, and dramatic. It is a space where we are loved individually and collectively, even if it comes at a cost. Unapologetically, the Black Church funeral is filled with expression—our hurt and pain with the singing and the praises unto God with the voice of triumph, "Hallelujah Anyhow!" Holloway cites a family who expressed that if we must send Momma home "we are going to do it in style." While others may say that this style represents drama and theatrics, these acts signify that "you mattered to us" and is a way to honor in death what was not always shown in life.

"African Americans have always used death material culture to resist; using last rites as a tool to subvert the racist, stereotypical caricature of thug and brute," Dr. Kami Fletcher tweets. However, such spending of a large amount of money on funeral and burial expenses can be problematic from a Christian point of view. In general, if we can *afford* an expensive casket for our deceased loved one, that is what we seek to provide. In some Black communities and urban subcultures, thick heavy weighted gold chains and gold teeth are expressions or symbols of riches and having one's head above water. It may be difficult to get Blacks to not put their money in the ground (in a casket that many view as a no-return investment), because of stereotypical perceptions from long, systematic oppression and not wanting to be seen as not being able to *afford* a nice casket. But to show your money, your bling-bling or riches, has become a trend in music videos that belittles the concept of quiet achievement. Such an approach to aesthetics with surface-level thinking and the display of capitalism keeps the practice of deeper thinking, sustainable practices, and long-term investment far from reach. However, a display of wealth is not the equivalent of beauty, yet the consideration of beauty—from both a Christian and an ecological point of view—must be at work regarding what is placed in or returned to the ground. We must consider the impact on the environment and creation and how all this relates to our discipleship, faithfulness, holiness, and commitment to God.

North Carolina Black Church funerals are filled with cultural significance and hold the power to bring people together—to *re*-member and to unify. For the Black Church, the funeral allows for space to honor God; and for the community, it creates an opportunity to honor Black life in an American context that has historically enslaved, oppressed, and ignored the value of Black life. In this space and place where Black people are devalued, Black Church funerals—with the funeral home and the church working together—are acts of agency, healing, *re*-membering, and resistance that push against the suppression of part of American culture.

Challenges for the Black Church Funeral: Ecological Effects of Contemporary Funeral Practices

Black Church funeral practices may have an African flare yet have adopted Westernized behaviors that are, for example, expensive and not ecologically sensitive. The Westernized funeral industry is not one that nourishes the planet but one that promotes human exceptionalism. Its model rests on the protection, sanitation, and beautification of the corpse, promoting the protection of the corpse from the ground by mounting barrier levels made of concrete, metals, and hardwoods. Alexandra Harker in *Landscapes of the Dead: An Argument for Conservation Burial*, reports the following:

> *Contemporary funeral practices and cemeteries are ecologically problematic. Digging in a modern cemetery in the United States is much like digging through a toxic waste site. Every year in the United States, the chemicals and materials buried along with bodies in a conventional burial include approximately 30 million board feet of hardwoods, 2,700 tons of copper and bronze, 104,272 tons of steel, and 1,636,000 tons of reinforced concrete (Greensprings Natural Cemetery Preserve, 2011). Exposure to formaldehyde affects funeral workers' health, demonstrated by a high incidence of leukemia and brain and colon cancer among embalmers (Holness, 1989). The pollutants are not limited to the area revealed elevated concentrations of metals used in casket construction, including copper, lead, zinc, and iron (Spongberg and Becks, 2000).*

Unclean and Polluted—The Funeral Industry Models: Roles, Rituals, and Routines

For the Black community, the experience is no different. How you *lay your loved one away* says a lot about you. Did you prepare for death? Was there an insurance policy? Where is the funeral? What casket can be afforded? and What is on display? At the time of death, no one wants to appear ill-prepared but instead *having their stuff together*, especially when it comes to the cost of the funeral. Consequently, the Black funeral home and the Black Church must accept the fact that they have bought into the commercialization of death and dying. In what ways have the Black Church and the Black funeral home industry become hazardous material handlers or, at a minimum, enablers of the carriers of hazardous materials?

The Embalming Process: Invoking Toxicity

The Federal Trade Commission (FTC) has a funeral rule that states that there is no state law that requires embalming for every death. Yet, Candi Cann shares that "funeral homes typically consider embalming the cornerstone of the funeral package, as embalming the deceased body generally means that visitation will be held." According to the Green Burial Council (GBC) embalming is "the process of removing blood and fluids from the dead body and inserting preservatives, surfactants, solvents, and coloration to slow decomposition and improve looks for a period of up to two weeks. Organs are punctured and drained of fluid with the use of a sharp instrument called a trocar; waste is disposed of in a standard septic system or municipal wastewater treatment plant." Embalming is not for long-term preservation of the body but to temporarily preserve the body using chemical injections and topical applications to maintain a life-like appearance and provide the family time to complete funeral preparations, make travel plans, and complete a viewing and other rituals or funeral obligations.

Although formaldehyde is the most preferred method of embalming, "The World Health Organization, and the U.S. Environmental Protection Agency, classify formaldehyde as a hazardous waste being a human carcinogen." Victoria J. Haneman, in "Tax Incentives for Green Burial," tells us that:

> *Embalming fluid is a solution used to temporarily preserve a corpse after death. Embalmers inject at least 3 gallons (11.3 liters) of the fluid into the cadaver's arterial system and body cavity to slow decay for wakes, funerals and other traditions that precede a burial. Embalming fluids often contain a combination of formaldehyde, chemicals like methanol and ethanol, and water. Formaldehyde can comprise up to 50 percent of a typical embalming fluid. Outside the funeral home, formaldehyde is*

> *used in medical labs as a tissue preservative and in pesticides and fertilizers. It's also a flammable, strong-smelling gas that's released from a variety of sources—cigarettes, exhaust pipes and building materials among them—and a known carcinogen.*

Today, ecologically friendly embalming options—with less-toxic chemicals and plant-based oils, refrigeration, and direct cremation without viewing with immediate burial—are within reach. Although more ecologically friendly embalming solutions have been marketed, formaldehyde, even though highly toxic, is the preferred method because of the sustained practices still used by the Black funeral industry.

Soil and Water Contamination

Soil and water contamination is of concern for environmentalists. Although most prevalent in older cemeteries, the soil and water contamination from funeral practices is disturbing. On one hand, the Pan American Health Organization says there is "little evidence of microbiological contamination of groundwater from burials." Yet, on the other hand, in a handful of cases adjacent to historical cemeteries, tests show elevated levels of contamination. It is "highly likely that the problems were caused by leachate from casket, vault, or embalming fluid or other incidental materials," Lee Webster suggests. Thus, there are soils that are not totally clean or unpolluted. But to what extent does the funeral industry, as cocreators of the earth, have in the management of the body and responsibility in the wellness of the soil?

Caskets and the Economics Continued

"African American people believe in funerals," says LaTrese Adkins. But the pressing question is: "How are we going to pay for it?" At death, many Black families struggle to answer this question. Often the ecclesial leader helps to guide the family not only through the funeral process but through tough questions regarding pricing. Because of long-standing communal relationships and church membership, often the church makes accommodations or adjustments to their offerings to meet the needs of the family. As stated earlier, Black funeral operating procedures and protocols have not changed and are considered old-fashioned. This brings to light the lack of variation in death options that is being offered to Black families.

Caskets (or coffins) are big business for funeral homes, says a local North Carolina Black-owned funeral home mortician and director. Ranging between $2,000 and $10,000, caskets have been the center of the business model for decades. Mark Harris tells of upsells and the sale of bells and whistles such as golden casket handles that often are sold as scrap metal. It is difficult for old school funeral directors and morticians to make a shift in longstanding business models. Investing in a crematory was initially a tough sell for this well-known funeral director and his father, the business founder. The thought was that the shift to cremations would kill business. The father believed that if the public were aware of the less expensive route in funeral processing, then the public would seek a way to reduce costs, and this would cut into the profits of the funeral home. However, the son has found that with the increase in demand for cremations over the past decade, their business has not suffered losses but is able to welcome the cremation market and not turn those seeking cremation away to other local businesses. Cremation took a while to catch on in the Black community. But now that it has, cremation has become a common consideration inside of funeral options.

There remain other opportunities inside of the Black funeral industry for environmentally friendly practices. The national funeral industry projected domestic annual revenues of $68 billion (by 2023) and, interestingly, the industry has slowly started to go green. A survey conducted by the National Funeral Directors Association (NFDA) found that 53.8 percent of respondents were interested in green burial options. Although death will come to every living organism on the planet, the green disposal of one's corpse remains a topic rarely discussed. This is where the Black funeral industry can be of service to its community and to the world.

Table 2.2. National Median Cost of an Adult Funeral with Viewing and Burial: 2019 vs. 2014.

Item	**2019**	**2014**	**% Change**
Non-declinable basic services fee	$2,195	$2,000	9.8%
Removal/transfer of remains to funeral home	$350	$310	12.9%
Embalming	$750	$695	7.9%
Other preparation of the body	$255	$250	2.0%
Use of facilities/staff for viewing	$425	$420	1.2%
Use of facilities/staff for funeral ceremony	$500	$495	1.0%
Hearse	$340	$318	6.9%
Service car/van	$150	$143	4.9%
Printed materials (basic memorial package)	$175	$155	12.9%
Metal burial casket	$2,500	$2,395	4.4%
Median Cost of a Funeral with Viewing and Burial	$7,640	$7,181	6.4%
Vault	$1,495	$1,327	12.7%
Total with vault	$9,135	$8,508	7.4%

According to the NFDA's 2019 General Price List Study, funeral costs are not rising as fast as the rate of inflation, but funerals are hardly inexpensive, as Table 2.2 shows.

But even a little increase can impact those in poverty. During the Great Depression people were "paying for funerals with livestock—pigs, chickens, and sometimes even artwork." Let us reclaim our funerals by paying attention to death ahead of time and creating plans that work best for our unique families owning a sense of agency.

Traditional Cremation

More popular in the white community, the trend toward cremation has been slow for members of the Black Church. Yet, by 2035, the rate of cremation in all fifty states is expected to exceed 50 percent, according to the NFDA. According to Mark Freeman, baby-boomers prefer a simpler, less expensive funeral, and therefore we have seen the number of cremations rise.

> *Between 1996 and 2000, cremations rose by five percentage points to 26% of the about 2.4 million deaths annually in the U.S., according to the Cremation Association of America, which sees no sign of the trend abating. By 2010, cremations are expected to account for 39% of American funerals, according to the association's data, and by 2025, the number should rise to about 48%. The average funeral with a casket and burial vault costs about $5,300, giving the funeral home a profit of about $750. A cremation, including the urn, costs about $2,600, with the funeral home making a profit of about $600. A cremation with no service or urn costs about $1,000.*

The uptrend in cremations is in line with a local white-owned funeral home in Raleigh, North Carolina that reports 80 percent of their business is cremation. They acknowledge that having a crematory was once thought of as a negative and would decrease business and income. However, they soon discovered that many customers wanted cremation, and for this Raleigh business having a crematory enhances their business options. As stated previously, cremation took a while to catch on in Black communities. But now that it has, cremation has become a common funeral option.

In many ways, African Americans are genuinely concerned with the land and their relationship with it. Separated and uprooted from their homelands, African Americans struggle to discern a sense of place and develop an attachment to land and earth. However, this concern with the land is often presented as having a historical or cultural nature, rather than an ecological, or better yet, a theological one.

Black ecclesial leaders can do better in the preparation of congregants and can shape how the community might think about their final resting places, informing members how to be better stewards of creation as we prepare to return to the ground. However, one can argue for the importance of having a more thorough and effective educational outreach for ecclesial leaders around ecological theology to address the silence. If, for example, someone does not know what is wrong, how can they be criticized for their action or the lack thereof? Given the oppression of Black Americans, it seems understandable that attention to theological ecology may not be a pressing issue just as it is not, so far, for most of the church. Notably, some Black ecclesial leaders seem to be silent on topics such as the link between theology, the earth, and our return to it—choosing to focus mainly on the soul and not the body or the whole of creation. The ecclesial leader would do well to keep the whole in mind. Yet, silence by the church leaders varies from being ill-informed to negligent. In the 1990s, the African American ministerial association partnered with a white-owned multinational funeral home chain to appoint preachers as "grief counselors," but this partnership was largely driven by interest in profit through the sale of grave materials. While Holloway may not be able to provide itemized documentation about her conclusion, still, she concludes that, "not surprisingly, the local pastors, their state and national denominational affiliates profited from the kickbacks of each sale." While some leaders are silent in order to profit from environmentally harmful funeral practices, others fail to consider the importance of our created bodies within a larger context. Could removing the silence possibly expose shamefulness of past sins where we have failed to act? Could we be unsure how to manage or to hold the tension together toward better? Moreover, overcoming silence moves the Black Church to pay attention to wellness and well-being of all creation, which in turn, invites making healthier choices, less manufactured processed ways of being, and solicits the building of new aesthetics. While identifying misplaced beauty might be seen as low hanging fruit, by naming this misplaced aesthetic, the Black Church will be guided, even more, toward wellness and wholeness found in truth and what really matters to God.

Through embracing conventional funeral practices, the Church has not exemplified good stewardship when it comes to the end of life. Now, however, the Black Church must extend the care of self toward the care of earth.

Cultural Perceptions and Societal Pressures: Bells and Whistles, Style, and Class

Walter Brueggemann argues in *The Prophetic Imagination* that "the task of prophetic ministry is to nurture, nourish, and evoke a consciousness and perception alternative to the consciousness and perception of the dominant culture around us." As the Black Church attempts to extend the care of self toward the care of earth, cultural perceptions appear to be challenging and accountability problematic. Challenges might include the social injustices of race and place, as well as accessibility and accountability. Regarding accountability, there is a closeness and an intimacy that exists between the Black Church and the Black funeral industry. Both pastors and morticians encounter people at pivotal and even vulnerable times, providing complementary services. Used properly, this relationship creates an opportunity for the church leader to inform the funeral industry and move them toward ecological justice.

Regrettably, Black churches have often watched silently and participated in the toxicity of funerals and funeral processions. On many levels, we make referrals and handoffs but leave creation-care for all unaccounted for. I contend that this is a mistake. If handoffs (partnerships) are being made, then the Black church is obligated to hold some responsibility and accountability. If ecclesial leaders allocate attention to the practices of the funeral home, especially as it relates to pollution and toxic practices, not only will this raise awareness in the community, but the environment will benefit from a collective communal effort instead of a single effort.

In *The Glad Funeral,* I recognize that there is "a slothfulness in addressing new funeral trends, with the need to balance the desire to be current, yet also to be respectful of tradition." Society can respect the notion not to move too quickly regarding cultural and traditional norms. However, the silence about harmful practices on the part of clergy has been allowed to continue under the pretense of not knowing or fully understanding the damage that is being done. There may be some truth to ignorance as the details of industry practices might not be widely known by nonspecialists.

In *The Glad Funeral,* I say that "theoretically, all funerals may be remarkably similar and uniform in appearance, yet behind the scenes, the local church exerts great effort to provide services for the family, at times with only days or a week's notice. While there are variations in funeral practices, there is a mindset that makes all the difference in a funeral being executed to witness God's Kingdom." The mindset of the church official or the funeral director carries a great deal of weight, authority, and leadership to a family in search of direction. I say that "the church, along with the funeral home, will work to deliver services that best meet the needs of the family." And that "Church officials can embody Christ's Kingdom." But how often are these services best for (Christ's) creation?

Culture and traditions come with societal pressures even at death. Corinna Schuler in "AIDS Crisis a Boom for the Funeral Industry" allows us to peek into the poverty and the booming business of funerals in Africa. In the face of poverty, fancy funerals with *a festive swing* include big hats, miniskirts, platform shoes, and cellphones—all on display. Schuler states that "African funerals are always a community affair where people come uninvited; although some just want the food." The funeral homes provide eight wheeled luxury vehicles (super-stretched limousines) with a beverage bar. From African culture to African American culture, Black funeral homes have standards to uphold. Historically, whether good or bad, these standards are passed on to the family; because at the time of such a public event, there is no family that does not wish to be seen in the best light, even in the face of poverty.

Before we get inside the doors of a Black church's funeral, profound expectations exist—no touching the *preserved* beautified body; the body must be enclosed in a casket; at the cemetery, the casket must be enclosed in a vault. Why aren't these expectations and the consequences that follow from these practices discussed and acted upon? Black churches aid in the separation (lack of closeness) to what is known or perceived to impact the environment. Nonbiodegradable coffins, embalming, and the *investment* of thousands of dollars in funerals offers the perception that being natural inside of a funeral is not popular, is not classy, and is not beautiful.

In general, when a family comes to or calls the church regarding a [pending] death, they are informed about the church funeral processes. Then, if asked, the church will direct the family to a funeral home to address other business that will occur outside of the church building. At times, the lines between church business and funeral home business may be blurred. However, this book argues for the ecclesial leader to engage early in the process and educate the church and community on funeral practices that may harm us and the environment.

African American Environmentalism: A Crisis of Culture and an Argument of Home—Ownership, Responsibility and Accountability

In America, a case can be made that African Americans embody the essence of environmentalism. Our ancestors and "slaves lived closer to the ground and often understood southern crops and environment better than their masters. . . . Nature uncultivated provided both highway and sanctuary for slaves," proclaims Mart A. Stewart in *To Love the Wind and the Rain: African Americans and Environmental History.* Yet, Norman Wirzba states that "when we talk about something like an environmental crisis, we need to understand that what we are really dealing with is a crisis of culture, a failure to be properly at home, and a distortion of what it means to be embodied beings living (necessarily and beneficially)." The environmental crisis is not foreign but is as close to us as our "Westernized" culture allows; and that the perceived proximity or closeness of the crisis is a factor in human behavior, our acts, or responses to it. How might "crisis of culture" be intersected with the way the Black community advocates for the preservation, restoration, or improvement of the natural environment (Black environmentalism)? Is the case for "failure to be properly at home," however plausible, being made by the very empowered population and capitalistic culture that strips one from *home* and from *roots*? This toxicity (crisis of culture), in and of itself, is a priority for many in the Black community and needs continued focus where justice is applied. Westernized culture, which contains systemic oppression, now leads environmental crisis efforts. Yet many refuse to take ownership of past and current toxic behavior toward other humans and miss opportunities to better manage or bridge past wrongdoings toward the direction of ecological justice to include justice for all—a cause that for the Church is covenantally right and holy. In this complex arena of environmentalism, since it has been said that the relationship between the Black

Church and environmental issues is one of complexity, might the ideology of "home" be a critical factor and barrier in the psychology of the Black community?

I was struck by the reference to being "properly at home" by Wirzba because of the displacement from home of Black and Brown bodies. Where is home for them? Is home where you were born? Is home wherever your parents are? Is it the street, the building, or the covering of wherever you lay your head? For the Christian, home is ultimately with God—where God abides. Yet, with urban renewal and now gentrification disrupting the Black community, where does the Black Church find itself? To what degree does this paradoxical relationship of home and land hold true for the Black community and its church? What can be done now to bring justice and peace to the earth? As resident aliens, the Black Church is to embody and be a representative of what we want the world to be regardless of the current land that is occupied.

In my dissertation, *Telerobotic Operator Risk-Taking Behavior* (2009), I studied the effects of remote operators who managed the site of hazardous material. I concluded that the operators, stewards of skilled mastery, who were at a distance from the material they were handling and thus having a greater protection level, exhibited greater risk-taking behavior regarding the hazardous situation than those who operated locally and on site. In other words, the operator's decision-making proved to be riskier in any emergency when the threat did not appear to be proximate. Thus, my research showed that there is a correlation between distance (whether perceived or actual) and behavior, which affects outcomes and consequences. Might this theory of distance be applied to the barriers—the synthetic coffins and other nonbiodegradable materials—used by the Black Church and its community, as well as the funeral industry as an indication of a lack of closeness (whether perceived or actual) to the environment, creation, and God? Are the funeral practices of Black Churches complicit with the environmental problems of traditional funeral practices in the United States? Might my risk-taking behavioral theory regarding distance be applied to the distance or lack of closeness the Black community (and the Black Church) may feel in relation to the environment (home); and therefore, projecting more risky behavior toward it?

But now, for the sake of our environment and for the sake of covenant, the Black Church must strike a balance between past and future; be bold in the recognition that the earth and the environment does not belong to the white community who "for five-hundred years have acted as if they owned the world's resources," and have held the beautiful resources (i.e., the trees) against us, against its neighbor. But for the Black Church, to make the greater psychological shift and argument for our earth conservation is not up for debate. Although, an argument can be made that the culture of the African American church and its community have been negatively impacted by the majority, Western capitalistic society, we all are responsible for the environment's care, and no one can leave it up to one group to act as good stewards. The Black Church did not create the environmental crisis nor is it our fault, but it is our fight.

Climate Change: It's Not Our Fault but It Is Our Fight

"Climate change is now a very familiar phrase but many of us are just beginning to understand its impact," according to the National Council of Churches USA: Eco Justice Programs. They argue that "African American churches have historically accepted the responsibility to address problems that have a negative impact on our communities." Yet James Cone asserts that "the leadership of the African America churches turned its much-needed attention toward ecological issues in the early 1990s." Did not the community follow? If not, why not? Dr. Betty Holley, executive committee member of Creation Justice Ministries, and Associate Professor of Ecological Theology at Payne Theological Seminary—the oldest freestanding African American seminary in the United States—makes the claim that the Black Church has an opportunity to reclaim the goodness of the land. Holley, a champion for ecological justice, suggests that attentiveness to the global climate is an invitation to pursue ecological conversion—a deep theological transformation "of being" in relation to our environment.

James Cone argues that ecology touches every sphere of human existence, and that Black liberation theology includes the fight for justice for life in all forms. Yet, this does not imply that the poor have no agency in the present global crisis, Michael Northcott in *A Moral Climate* suggests. For example, considering creation and the earth as we return to it by changing the way in which we are buried respects the notion that our last act on earth should not be to harm the earth. A commitment to being environmentally friendly requires that the scope of all human activity be integrated into the biosphere in a way that is sustainable.

Yet, how central is environmental justice to the Black Church? Because of the perception that the climate does not present an acute situation, the Black community will more than likely find itself acting in a reactionary way once environmental harms hit home. Studies have found that Blacks are less informed, less aware, and therefore less concerned with environmental issues than whites. Often the Black Church and Black communities are living in a reactive world instead of being proactive based on what is known. To a degree, reluctance due to mistrust is understandable because those who lead in the effort to eradicate global warming are identified with the same people in power who led such efforts as urban renewal and gentrification.

But will the Black community embrace greening in death? It would be helpful for the Black Church to make a public confession and release a statement of change regarding its stance and efforts to be faithful stewards of God's resources in caring for the planet. Holley thinks that the Black Church and its community should be held accountable for our actions and practices. Holley notes:

> *Our economic woes, social unease, and environmental depletion are being shaken to the core due to our misplaced purposes and values of the whole of God's creation. Our relationship with wealth and possession has become corrupt and idolatrous. We have been seeking happiness through things rather than through relationships. Too often we, in the church, have mimicked the values of wider society.*

With this statement, Holley urges the church to take responsibility for its actions and practices toward a better environment, toward a healthy creation.

The Black Church cannot be blamed for the environmental crisis—although it has, like almost all peoples, contributed to it—but it is our responsibility to help fix it. Given the crisis we are facing, this may "cause one to repent from our habits and practices of undisciplined management. This call to repentance is particularly urgent now that we have knowledge about the fragility of ecosystems and the disproportionate negative impact environmental calamities exact on the poor who are least responsible for them."

It is crucial for the Black Church to be attentive to climate change, global warming, and environmental protections. Fred Bahnson, in Ellen Davis's *Getting Involved with God*, tells us that "reverence for the earth and reverence for God cannot be separated." Bahnson furthers the claim by highlighting that "soil is not dirt. It is a living organism, or rather, a collection of organisms, and it must be fed. Soil both craves life and wants to produce more life, even a hundredfold." On those same lines, Norman Wirzba argues that soil is a complex web of relationships that represents a deeply mysterious bridge, while Willie Jennings extends the conversation on eco-theology with a racial-ethnic component. In an interview on environment justice, Jennings teaches that "race and place are two sides of the same coin. When you turn land into dirt, you can then turn people into racists." For example, too often industrial waste is buried in the ground next to poor communities (communities of color), who then are more likely to be affected by pollution, and subject to a higher percentage of health concerns. An eco-theological vision of God's creation, according to Jennings, is "tied to identity, [and] that to understand who they were, you understand where they were." We humans need to begin to see ourselves as organically related to the rest of creation.

The environmental crisis creates an opportunity for the Black Church to take ownership and assume our place at the table regarding global issues. We declare to be intentional about entering and embracing global conversations and making global impacts. We understand that what we do locally impacts what occurs globally. Therefore, we are committed to identifying areas of impact where we are accountable and can make a difference. We seek to lead the church in global sustainability by implementing healthier practices that takes all creation into account. To extend the conversation, Holley says that attentiveness to the global climate issue is an invitation to pursue ecological conversion to ultimately protect our *home*, earth.

Black Environmentalism: The White and Black Pathways of Race and Place

As global researchers, scientists, and US Congressional leaders propose ways to combat climate change, where is the Black church voice? With the overwhelming scientific consensus about climate change's projected harms, to what extent does the Black church take ownership in making a collective contribution toward environmental awareness and sustainability? The church can be a leader in fostering such awareness and offering advice regarding practical environmental issues, such as burial and the proper use of resources.

Studies on the environment and the Black community have shown the Black community tends to be less involved in environmental issues than the white community. Dorceta Taylor in "Blacks and the Environment" would suggest that the association with the Black community and the environment is complex. Taylor conducted an extensive study on Blacks and the environment and attempted to break down possible reasons for the gap between Black and white involvement regarding the environmental issues. Taylor not only details possible explanations for the gaps or the Black community's lack of concern and activity regarding environmental issues and notes the role of the following factors: solidarity, cognitive perception of reality, resources, and psychological factors. Taylor also points out that "the environmental movement could attract more Blacks through an expansion of the civil rights agenda to include environmental issues." By mixing and joining the things that already appeal to the Black community, environmental concerns would become more of a priority. Similarly, I seek to join environmental concerns with a foundational principle of the Black Church—covenantal relationship—in hopes of keeping the environmental crisis on its frontal lobe.

Why should an element of race factor in the conversation of an environment in crisis? Michael Northcott in *A Moral Climate* extends the conversation directly toward climate change. Northcott informs us that "humans are in effect in charge of the climate of the planet. This is an important point, and one that too many Christians—both Black and white—have ignored. Yet Global warming disproportionately impacts the poor," with a high percentage of the poor being people of color. Philip J. Landrigan in the *Mount Sinai Journal of Medicine* informs us that environmental injustice is "the inequitable and disproportionately heavy exposure of poor, minority, and disenfranchised populations to toxic chemicals and other environmental hazards." Environmental injustice is highly correlated with other factors that link poverty to poor health, including inadequate access to medical and preventive care, lack of safe play spaces for children, lack of access to healthful foods, absence of good jobs, crime, and violence. Hazardous exposures in the environment are potent causes of disease, disability, and death in persons of all ages and especially in infants and children. Landrigan cites a few factors that are worth repeating here:

> *Environmental injustice contributes to disparities in health status across populations of different ethnic, racial, and socioeconomic backgrounds, such as differences in the incidence and prevalence of asthma (doubled in frequency since 1980), obesity resulting in diabetes (41% of 5-year-old children entering kindergarten in the 5 boroughs of New York City most prevalent in African American and Latino children), lung cancer, and a range of mental health and developmental problems (pre-term birth increased 27% since 1981; neurodevelopmental disorders such as mental retardation and attention deficit/hyperactivity affect 5% to 10% of the 4 million babies each year in the United States).*

Given that the environmental movement could attract more Blacks through an expansion of the civil rights agenda to include environmental issues (Taylor), our approach cannot simply be to hand-over and to be hands-off but to still lean in and to be a partner in the crisis, in the struggle. With the hands-off approach, the Black Church and people of color have been negligent (a too risky position) in our behavior toward the environment and global sustainability issues. We can do more.

In recent decades, we have all been encouraged to participate in recycling, in which Black families across America have played their part. From the kitchen—the center of the house—we have chosen to participate in local city recycling initiatives, correctly taking care of our plastics and glass, and the proper handling of hazardous materials. Yet, as James Cone in "Whose Earth Is It Anyway?" suggests, "people of color are not treated seriously, that is, as if they have something essential to contribute to the conversation." Cone argues that ecology touches every sphere of human existence, and so he expands his Black liberation theology to include not only the fight for justice for life but also the ecological efforts to create a mutual ecological dialogue. He aims to have the Black voice taken seriously inside of conversations about the environment and asks, "How can we create a genuinely mutual ecological dialogue between whites and people of color if one party acts as if they have all the power and knowledge?" He recognizes the problem that the Black Church is not asked to the table when decisions are being made on such matters. I agree with Cone's assertions because having representation already at the table presents a greater magnitude to attract others of like kind to join and to get involved. So, Cone thus gives impetus to the reclaiming of the earth as our home and encourages the Black Church and its community that it can speak to and live out this environmental embodiment.

The COVID-19 pandemic encouraged Americans to go outdoors to walk with the touch of the sun on the face and the coat of the wind around the shoulders. The Black Church has a complicated connectedness to the environment, whether by force or by nature. Cassandra Johnson and Josh McDaniel in "Turpentine Negro" speak of the woods as sanctuary and a pathway to freedom for the enslaved. Dianne Glave in "Rural African American Women, Gardening, and Progressive Reform in the South" expands our diversified look in the African American story by capturing the beauty of planting, flowers, and gardening for many African American women. Yet American environmentalism, with its Western way of thinking and of being, has found a way to capitalize and to lure society away from such natural beauty. Often, the Black community looks to what can be bought more than what is natural, the shinier the better. Thus, the Black Church is obligated to help us find a path to what is right and true.

Even though at times there are feelings of despair, the Black Church must stay focused on the work that is to be done before Christ returns. This means not forsaking the earth. Even though this world is not our eternal home, God has graciously given us the earth as home and has made us one with it. Therefore, we cannot overlook the way in which we should be in harmony with the earth.

Strengthening the Marriage Between the Black Church and the Environment: Toward a New Aesthetic in Black Environmentalism

The Black community values its aesthetic genius, and some in the church consider this aspect of Black life to be sacred. Theologian Kenyatta Gilbert in *Exodus Preaching* suggests that the sacred encompasses the realities of God, revealed truths, and highest moral values. There is still a more excellent way for the Black Church that requires a reclaiming of that highest moral ethic. Yet, this higher moral ethic comes at a cost—the trading of the shiny (temporal) for the eternal. Our aesthetic genius is more fully realized when it is aligned with the will of God.

The Black Church already holds the key to strengthening its relationship with the environment through the principle of covenantal relationship. By embodying commitment and love for the surrounding community and the environment (its neighbors), the Black Church has the potential to be widely recognized as a womb, a center, and the soul of the community. If we see creation as beautiful and precious, as God does, it will determine how we use the environment or interact with it. Conversely, how we care for creation impacts how beautiful the Church is before God.

It can be argued that if the love that one shares is not precious than the question can be posed, Is it love? Our treatment of earth—how we think about and care for earth—if not precious (pure and holy), is problematic. In our funeral practices, we have an opportunity to embrace a new aesthetic that is aligned with God's estimation of and care for creation. Ellen Davis argues that "holiness in Leviticus is not primarily the quality of individuals; holiness is the character of a community observing a comprehensive pattern of life that is healthful and harmonious." I extend Davis's argument by stating that a pure (holy) treatment of earth is a show of thanks and certainly a show of love.

How best to argue persuasively for the reimagining, reclaiming, and creating of a new aesthetic between the Black Church and the environment? Forged in solidarity, the Black Church has always emphasized and engaged in social services, now it can help the Black community reclaim its grounding and freedom in relation to the environment. One approach is to look to the Black Church and its ecclesial leaders to partake in and then take ownership of this movement. The Black Church is historically a place of unification, strength, and purpose. Victor Anderson in "The Black Church and the Curious Body of the Black Homosexual," tells us that despite its issues, "the Church is one place where our public and private commitments meet. Sometimes they meet in agreement and sometimes not." According to Eric Lincoln and Lawrence Mamiya in *The Black Church in the African American Experience*, the Black Church "has no challenger as the cultural womb of the Black community." To what extent is this concept still valid? Christopher J. Beeley describes "the *soul* as the center of a person's life—our values, commitments, and choices, our thoughts and feelings, our memories and hopes for the future." Although historic by nature, might the Black Church be a place of centering and guidance, despite its issues? Anderson would agree that many still stay and seek to forge a better tomorrow even if the Black Church appears to be the church of their yesterday. God is still birthing and speaking through the Black Church's womb, and it is important for the community to listen. I argue that it is from this womb that better practices of environmental and ecological awareness can be forged even better than before. With this stance, the Black Church can gain (or reclaim) a foot inside of the hopes and dreams of its people. Today we can start anew.

A More Excellent Way

All of this presents real challenges for the Black Church that desires to exhibit a strong ecological faith. Black Church funerals have contributed to the starvation and the polluting of the soil. The funeral industry models create space for the morticians, ecclesial leaders, and even grieving families to become hazardous material handlers; and to participate as pollutants of the earth. The handling of the body as it decomposes—whether in a tomb, mausoleum, grave, earth, or water, or by exposure to the elements or by carrion-consuming animals—should be viewed in relation to creation.

In addition to starvation and the polluting of the soil, aided by the funeral industry, the Black Church has aided in the defining of what is beautiful or an acceptable bar for honoring the dead. In the house of the Lord, there has been no push back on the beautification of the dead, the delaying of the natural decaying process of embalming methodologies, synthetic coffins, paints and materials, or the cost of such practices. Because the church is very much a part of the funeral industry with its congregants also funeral home personnel, the funeral industry has been allowed to function in the church without questions or regulations regarding a better way or of strengthening one covenant (to God through the environment) in a way that is reflective in its practices. The Black community understands, loves and is forever appreciative to our Black morticians. Yet, *The Green Funeral* simply seeks to challenge all to be more environmentally friendly as we serve the present age.

As *The Green Funeral* seeks to point the Black Church in the direction of ecological sensitivity, the prevailing thought is that as we develop "our relationship with God, our materialistic values will be challenged and transformed." By making shifts in the point of view and behaviors inside the Black funeral, the Black Church can be successful toward embodying care for God's creation. Ellen Davis would call this having a healthy or a *wholesome materiality*—turning from rampant materialism—where your commitment to living with a holy awareness of what God loves is heightened. Let us honor the body even in death—both human bodies, living and dead, and the earth's "body." In life the human body is sacred and considered a temple. So, let us participate in death care in the most life-giving of ways as we give our loved ones back to God.

As we turn our attention to chapter 3, we look to empirical data that highlights many of the problems and concerns of the impact of traditional funeral practices on the environment and the larger community. We look deeper into how *carrying the load of the casket* might speak to other much larger predicaments involving the earth, ecological faith, and environmental justice.

3

Raised Awareness

GOD NEVER STOPS calling us toward God; and toward greater, even in death. Although the process may be lengthy for some and shorter for others; curvy for some and straight for others, the awareness gained (the raised awareness) cannot be bought with silver or gold. But the beauty in lived experiences makes salient the gifts that God has placed in each of us. The willingness to engage, to learn, and to grow in God highlights the beauty that is to be shared with and throughout creation. There is beauty in our interest in, our raised awareness of, and our strengthened resolve toward our covenant and commitment in and for the things of God without fear; however challenging things may become.

There was a time when I never thought that I would be in ministry. I was a skilled industrial engineer and spent the summer of 2008 in Lincoln, Massachusetts at the Massachusetts Institute of Technology (MIT). Well, from there I placed an MIT license tag on the front of my car. One day at a car wash a person asked, Are you a preacher? I almost said something that was not nice. Instead, I said, Why would you ask me that? The person replied, Because the tag on the front of your car reads MIT which means

Minister in Training. Well, obviously, the person did not look close enough to see that in smaller print behind the big MIT was Massachusetts Institute of Technology.

I was adamant about not being a minister. I knew my biological father was in ministry (which was a reason for me to run the opposite direction) and my mother was a missionary in the church; for me, ministry was not my thing. If there was an inkling that it might be a minister, I asked God to make it very plain and clear.

In 2010, before graduating from engineering school, I was diagnosed with breast cancer. I needed no other sign. When presented with such a serious critical illness where life and death hang in the balance, I needed no other tap. Yes, I wanted to be sure and yes there were fears to overcome—the fear of not being good enough; of not knowing Scripture like other ministers; the fear of missing out on fun and parties that I still wanted to do. As I look back over my life, there were fears along the way that I had to overcome.

There is beauty in the process, although the process can be difficult. Beauty is living a life that is in the will of God; then continuing that beauty in death into eternity is most desired.

The Beauty in Facing Your Fear

Military and Basic Training

> *Peace I leave with you, my peace I give unto you: not as the world giveth, give I unto you. Let not your heart be troubled, neither let it be afraid.*
> (John 14:27 KJV)

I wasn't always planning on ministry. Upon my graduation from high school, I saw that technology was bursting out as a new social force, showing itself in huge car phones and computer automation. I wanted so much to be a part of this new world, but I found college computer programming classes difficult. I struggled. I was placed on academic probation, and with my grandmother's passing, I was devastated. So, I left home in Fayetteville, North Carolina and went into the United States Army. In 1989, *I walked into basic training.* Fearful, I had butterflies in my stomach, still *I walked.* As soon as my feet crossed the threshold into basic, the drill sergeants began yelling at me and the others in my group. When I got a chance, I called my momma crying and told her what they were doing, how I was being treated. She told me to hang in there and that she was proud of me. I remember this call as the first time I heard my mother say she was proud of me. I completed my service, receiving an honorable discharge in April 1993.

The Beauty of Walking with Jesus: In Business as an Engineer

I will never leave thee, nor forsake thee. (Heb 13:5 KJV)

After my military service, I still wanted very much to be a part of the automation boom. It was such a far cry from the chicken coops and the cotton fields of my youth. The computer industry bore no resemblance to my typical Monday routine, hanging clothes on the line. Technology was my ticket to a new way of life. International Business Machines' (IBM) Big Blue and mainframes were all the rage. In 1996, I walked into IBM with butterflies in my stomach *but still I walked.* With the big computer giant, I navigated my way from city to city for the next eight years.

As part of my desire to continue learning, I later walked into MIT in the summer of 2008. At that time, *Business Insider* considered MIT one of the best colleges in America. I knew MIT's history before stepping through the door. Surely this reputation added to my butterflies. *Still, I walked.* I applied for an internship there anyway. That summer was one of the best of my life. I learned so much from the people I knew at MIT, some of the best and the brightest I had ever met. I also enjoyed running alongside the Charles River every day. As I mentioned in the previous chapter, I even got an MIT license plate on my car.

Through another internship program, I began working at SAS, a data analytics firm in Cary, North Carolina. Again, I had butterflies in my stomach. In the summer of 2009, SAS was at the top of the list of *Fortune*'s best companies to work for in the United States, a position it continued to hold through 2010 and 2011. Regardless of the company's high standing, my butterflies never departed. I loved the atmosphere and the thought of being at a top company in the United States, but I missed something. Although I struggled with computer programming and settled for a testing environment, I had to fight to stay in the company's moving parts. Simultaneously, something inside of me was pointing to other opportunities. After I did all that I could do to stay, I declined another job offer in the company because the position was a rough fit. God used the rejection notices as divine shifts in direction and remained always present.

Duke Divinity

> *Study to shew thyself approved unto God, a workman that needeth not to be ashamed, rightly dividing the word of truth.* (2 Tim 2:15 KJV)

Now back to that fateful day at a car wash in Georgia, when a stranger asked me if I was a minister because of my MIT license plate and I said emphatically, "No, not me!" I didn't realize God's sense of humor and my preparation, even then, for a future in the ministry.

The stranger's comment came before I had any indication of a call, which would come specifically with my cancer diagnosis. Years later, honed by military service, my hard-working drive remained. I wanted to continue my education, so I enrolled at Duke Divinity School. I felt anxious that my background did not readily prepare me for divinity school. *Yet I walked.* God spoke these words to me: "I will use all of the preparation, all of the shifting and sifting, to position you best for your divine destiny." As a Duke seminarian, I was afforded relationship-building opportunities with folks from rural America and the largest metropolitan cities. My classmates and

I would fly to Durham, North Carolina to engage in and to exchange theologies of the Gospel, pedagogies, and practices. We would then return to our homes as wiser leaders ready to share with others, to implement new ideas and approaches, and to make a difference in our churches and communities.

As a seminarian, I learned to listen for the voice of the Lord as I sought discernment for God's people. God continues to speak. Now more than ever, I listen, read, and annotate stories as I engage in people's lives. Willie Jennings, then a Duke professor now a Yale professor, put it like this: "Our goal is to change the world we understand because we serve a God who has changed and is changing this world and invites us to yield ourselves to that changing power." As I share my uncomfortable story, people find comfort in common ground. I learned in divinity school, and in ministry, that the commonality of pain and suffering breaks down barriers between people. So let the voice of the Lord be inhabited, which calls us forward.

A big church pulpit has not been my regular preaching assignment. Instead, in nursing homes I build relationships, create a pulpit, and preach to those who are receiving medical care for life's effects on the body. These people often fall asleep and awaken with a soft touch as I offer a prayer and a blessing. I preach to them as if I were preaching to millions who are not on prescribed medication. However, they remember me, and they ask, "Are you the one who came before?" I touch them and reply "Yes, I am, so glad to see you again." Forward movement thinking and resolve in ministry breaks down barriers, even to the sick and those confined. Even now, in my first pastorate assignment, I still preach to thousands even if there are only five in the church building.

The Fear of Being Under Water and Baptism

> *And Jesus, when he was baptized, went up straightway out of the water: and, lo, the heavens were opened unto him, and he saw the Spirit of God descending like a dove, and lighting upon him: And lo a voice from heaven, saying, This is my beloved Son, in whom I am well pleased."* (Matt 3:16, 17 KJV)

I was afraid of being under water. The process of my life, from my work in the tech industry and career in the army to my ministry and basic acts such as eating and writing, have been marked by fear. While taking swimming lessons at the YMCA as a child, I feared the water so much that, when my turn came to jump in, I tried my best to jump on the instructor standing in the water. Unfortunately for me, she moved, and I had to be rescued from the bottom. Forty years passed before I would place my head under water by being fully submerged for water baptism.

I was raised in the Methodist church and was baptized with a sprinkling of water. I had not given much thought to baptismal methodology and was not taught extensively about its meaning. However, I had heard about the dirty pools of water where the old folks had been baptized. When I went to college and entered the Baptist church, I was exposed to full immersion baptism. Fearing deep waters, and new to the concept, I did not give full immersion much consideration. Since entering the ministry in the Baptist denomination, I found that local churches often require full immersion baptisms. I had to face my fears. Being intentional about going deeper and wider in the things of God meant that I had to face one of my greatest challenges—going under water. I sought the help of the Holy Spirit by fasting and praying (Matt 17:21). I took a leap of faith and agreed to be fully immersed.

The local church baptized every second Sunday. Candidates, including me, stood at the front of the church, behind the choir stand, and under the cross. The ministers waited in the water to baptize us. The music played loudly. "Do you believe in Jesus Christ? Do you believe that Jesus Christ died on the cross for your sins, was buried and rose again on the third day," the pastor asked. "Is it your intent to live a godly life?" I replied, "yes, yes, and yes!" Then the pastor said, "according to your confession of faith, I baptize you in the name of the Father, the Son, and the Holy Ghost." Before anyone could say "Amen," the minister quickly, with a strong arm, moved me under water. I was totally immersed! I felt my body go down farther in the water than I had wanted to go. Initially, I thought the tip of my nose would be the indicator of "far enough," but I felt my body go deeper than I would have ever placed myself. Then with another quick motion, the minister raised me out of the water. I heard the "Amens" and the applause from the pastor, the minister, and the congregation. As I was, symbolically, like Christ, raised from the dead in the newness of life, the water fell off my soaked body. I knew in my spirit that old things had passed away, that what should not have been attached to me had fallen away. I felt God doing a new thing in my life, even if I did not know what or how. I wanted to go deeper for Christ. My immersion became an image of the ways I would have to overcome fear, or let God help me overcome fear, in order to move ahead.

There is beauty in listening to the voice of God; beauty in living a life that is ordered by God. Beauty is living a life that is in the will of God then continuing that beauty in death into eternity. There is a raised awareness to knowing that God will never stop calling us toward greater, toward Godself, even in death. May we be more beautiful than ever before willingly engaging in, and with, creation in strengthening our resolve for the things of God without fear.

The Impact of Traditional Funeral Practices on the Environment

Lee Webster, formerly of the Green Burial Council and author of *Changing Landscapes*, offers this shocking analysis:

> *Each year in the U.S., 22,500 traditional cemeteries put roughly the following into our soil: a) 827,060 gallons of embalming fluid, 97.5 tons of steel, 2,028 tons of concrete, and 56,250 board feet of*

> *high-quality tropical hardwood in just one acre of land; b) Each cremation releases between .8 and 5.9 grams of mercury as bodies are burned. This amounts to between 1,000 and 7,800 pounds of mercury released each year in the U.S. 75% goes into the air and the rest settles into the ground and water; c) With embalmers at an 8+ times higher risk of contracting leukemia (Journal of the National Cancer Institute, 11.24.09) and a 3 times higher risk of ALS (Journal of Neurology, Neurosurgery & Psychiatry, 7.13.15), and (d) You could drive about 4,800 miles on the energy equivalent of the energy used to cremate someone—and to the moon and back 85 times from all cremations in one year in the U.S.).*

The impact of traditional funeral practices—embalming, cremations, and burials—is quite disturbing, especially when the church seeks first to do no harm. With such analysis, the Black Church can take inventory of its actions toward engaging in better funeral practices and taking better care of creation.

According to the National Funeral Director Association's (NFDA) annual Cremation and Burial Report, in 2020, the burial rate was 37.5 percent (down 7.7% from 2015) and projected cremation rate was 56 percent (up 8.1% from 2015). At the same time, air studies in North Carolina show air pollution to be of grave concern. John Clarence

Scarborough, III of Scarborough & Hargett Funeral Home in Durham, North Carolina, asserts that cremations in North Carolina are trending upward. However, he admits that white funerals are leading the way in cremations. Scarborough shares that Black funeral practices tend to be more old-fashioned, with, for instance, *viewings*—the display and observation of an embalmed body—continuing to remain in favor much longer. Nevertheless, there is no disputing that cremations are on the rise. Therefore, the attention to what is being put into the air (environment) remains of utmost concern. Dominique Mosbergen in "Death Has a Climate Change Problem" argues that concern about the environmental impact of conventional burials and cremations mounts.

The toxic environmental impact of traditional funeral practices needs to be considered by Black churches, for whom funeral rites and rituals are of great importance. Although shifts have been observed in the funeral industry in America (i.e., the creation of a "funeral director"; viewing deceased bodies at home versus conducting viewings at the funeral home; having more closed casket funerals), the *Wall Street Journal* contends that baby boomers are fiercely transforming the industry with the demand for simpler and far less expensive methods of funeralizing such as cremations. As seen in previous chapters, Black Church funerals have been preserved and, for most spiritual and practical purposes, have been slow to adaptation and change. Might economics be a factor in the slow adaptation to change? The *Wall Street Journal* continues: "'The average funeral with a casket and burial vault costs about

$5,300, giving the funeral home a profit of about $750. A cremation, including the urn, costs about $2,600, with the funeral home making a profit of about $600. A cremation with no service or urn costs about $1,000." As seen with the rise in cremations, a change in practice would impact the financial models on which these businesses have been built. This is a logical rationale for resistance because more ecologically responsible funeral practices are less economically profitable given the current personal and material resources that support the current toxic models. Yet, the toxic environmental impact of traditional funeral practices can no longer be overlooked by Black churches, for whom funeral practices, rites, and rituals are critical. Traditional funeral practices with conventional burials and cremations are problematic:

1. Embalming injects chemicals into the deceased body, all the while, presenting a dangerous environment to the worker. Then the body is often cremated or buried.
2. During cremation, fossil fuels and toxic metals are released into the air at an alarming rate. Cremations are now the number one deathcare practice in the United States; and
3. Burial grounds are overtaxed by tons of synthetic materials, which prohibits plant life and reproduction. Burials are ranked second in deathcare practice in the United States.

The Ecological Crisis, Environmental Theology, and Ecological Faith

As we and our loved ones move toward death, we often turn toward God for comfort and hope. But do we think about God and how our death relates to God's created order—that is, to the environment? I will explore environmental theology—the ecology of God—to propose a revised approach to decisions about burials and deathcare, the consideration of products and the services relating to cremation, burials, and other processes of dying.

In the late 1960s, Rachel Carson in *Silent Spring* analyzed the impact that the distribution of chlorinated hydrocarbons had on animals and the environment. Today, climate change, accompanied by global warming, is a good example of an environmental crisis that impacts all. "The ecological crisis may be the most far-reaching theological crisis ever to confront the church," says Ellen Davis in *Getting Involved with God*. Although some may not agree with Davis's conclusion, the anticipated impact of climate change if humans don't act to cut carbon emissions are astronomical. "Human-induced climate change is already affecting many weather and climate extremes in every region across the globe," says United Nations Secretary-General Antonio Guterres in an Intergovernmental Panel on Climate Change (IPCC) report. The report further states that some of the changes may be irreversible, but "there is still time to limit climate change." The

IPCC urges our world leaders to act in attempts to keep our global warming temperature below 1.5 degrees Celsius and in efforts to avoid suffering additional extreme events such as exceptional heatwaves.

In addition to the problems created by climate change, breaking down the barriers to food production and eliminating the lack of proximity to preservation of food and the reliance on processed food is "the clarion call for people all over this earth," says Betty Holley. While the Black Church did not create the ecological crisis, it is not something the church can ignore. If we don't care for the land and thus our fellow humans in daily living, then how can we care about land amid dying?

Davis argues that "the fruitful yet fragile beauty of the fertile earth constitutes an ongoing call of responsibility, and for many of us, repentance, and a change of life." I suggest that how we (the Black Church) handle the dead contributes to injurious behavior toward the environment. Funeral industry practices are problematic because they pollute and reflect a perversion of our relationship with God because of the way that they seek to deny our "dustiness." The church has uncritically embraced these practices. This perversion starts well before the actual funeral day. It begins with the thought, or perception, that closeness to natural death and the decay that naturally follows is unhealthy. Candi Cann in "Black Deaths Matter: Earning the Right to Live" asserts that "embalming the deceased generally means that visitation will be held." This normalized practice creates a perception that a deceased body that is not embalmed cannot be gathered around. A lack of knowledge (and in some cases, simply, a lack of action) about the toxic impact of the funeral industry on the environment has impacted us all. Yet, the funeral industry has long benefited, or at minimum, relied on the sales of shiny caskets, embalming, and vaults that separate us from the ground and ultimately from a full, complete, and natural death and decomposition.

As I have already pointed out, funeral industry models create space for morticians, ecclesial leaders, and even grieving families to become hazardous material handlers and polluters of the earth, thereby compromising our faith and covenant with God. Within the Black Church, funerals are occasions when what is to be honored and what is "beautiful" is often polluted—hence the use of embalming, buying fancy coffins, etc. With the right vision that incorporates environmental concerns, what is thought of as "beautiful" can be seen as truly ugly, sinful, and disobedient. We can see these practices as acts of covetousness. In buying fancy coffins, we create idols of our wealth and dishonor our fathers and mothers in the process. Regarding such behavior, Everett Fox in *The Five Books of Moses* would suggest we look to Leviticus for revelation. Fox asserts that Leviticus 19 is rhetorically powerful and extends holiness to virtually every area of our lives to include ethics and relations (a) regarding land, plants, and animals, which are our neighbors. It matters how we engage our fellow non-human creatures; verse 18 says "you shall love your neighbor as yourself," and (b) between people. As Leviticus 19:1–5 states:

> *The Lord spoke to Moses, saying: Speak to all the congregation of the people of Israel and say to them: You shall be holy, for I the Lord your God am holy. You shall each revere your mother and father, and you shall keep my sabbaths: I am the Lord your God. Do not turn to idols or make cast images for yourselves: I am the Lord your God. When you offer a sacrifice of well-being to the Lord, offer it in such a way that it is acceptable in your behalf.*

Holiness not only involves the consideration of—how we *think of* then what we *do with*—our bodies but it also includes land. God's instructions to keep "my sabbaths" and in Leviticus 25:1–4 God instructs Israel to observe a sabbath rest of the land every seven years. In addition to Fox, Jacob Milgrom in *Leviticus: A Book of Ritual and Ethics* asserts that the holiness source (H) is where "the domain of the sacred expands, embracing the entire land, not just the sanctuary, and all of Israel, not just the priesthood." Milgrom speaks to Leviticus 25 and sabbath for the land where there is a need for land to take a rest toward redemption and growth. Milgrom declares that land sabbath is a complement to sacrifices. With sabbath, one can immediately give and get care for the land. If we are called to let the land rest, then surely that means we are to care for the land's health and not to pollute it. Likewise, no pollution is also comely for our dead bodies and the land. According to the precepts of Leviticus, caring for the health of the earth is holy and right, not just for the soil's sake, but for ours, as we are organically related covenant partners with the land. For today's church, there is a need for a change in thinking so that our understanding of covenant expands to include the whole of creation.

The Covenant Triangle—Let There Be No Separation Between You and the Dust of the Ground

"Reverence for the earth and reverence for God cannot be separated," argues Ellen Davis. God's covenantal relationship is with Israel (people), and the land. This bond cannot be separated. Indeed, there is a connectivity (a connectedness) that cannot be broken or separated; neither should space be forged between. To live out our covenantal destiny through attentiveness to our final return to the land is indeed beautiful. Creation is good and so we should not distance ourselves from it with barriers and pollutants. According to Davis, *adamah* represents fertile soil where God reached to the land to create an image of God. God loves the soil (land) and what God loves is valuable. We must love and be good stewards of what God loves. Unfortunately, this bond to creation is often broken and violated. It is not farfetched to view our lives as often not being attentive to, and at times, actively toxic toward what God loves, gifted, and covenanted: land. With an agrarian reading of the Bible, priority would be placed on the care of land. But if we seek to be attentive, obedient, and to strengthen our covenant relationship, then we should remember God's promise, "I will remember my covenant with Jacob; I will remember my covenant with Isaac, and also my covenant with Abraham, and I will remember the land" (Lev 26:40–46). With this covenantal language, Davis strongly suggests that we are obligated to be attentive to the inseparability of our reverence for the earth and for God.

Davis speaks to the covenantal triangle and how humans and the land are covenant partners with God and how they either flourish together or suffer together. Leviticus further extends the goodness theme with the joining of care—covenantal loyalty—with obedience.

> *If you follow my statutes and keep my commandments and observe them faithfully, I will give you your rains in their season, and the land shall yield its produce, and the trees of the field shall yield their fruit. Your threshing shall overtake the vintage, and the vintage shall overtake the sowing; you shall eat your bread to the full and live securely in your land. And I will grant peace in the land, and you shall lie down, and no one shall make you afraid.* (Lev 26:3–6)

Our toxic burial practices are but one example of humanity's mistreatment of creation that violates God's statutes to exercise proper dominion over the earth. These verses in Leviticus 26 highlight what is at stake. In our transgression we put ourselves in jeopardy of disrupting the earth's geological processes that make human life possible: regular rains and a healthy agricultural system. But if we seek to be obedient, to strengthen our conventual relationship, and to better care for creation then we shall reap the benefits of rain and fruit and shall lie down without fear.

Humanity, especially our church leaders, is called to the ground literally and figuratively, to be in covenant too with the land. Yet, we have broken the covenant by overlooking our toxic behavior. Davis acknowledges this as a violation of covenant (disobedience) and *the undoing of the world*. Thus, causing all of creation to suffer.

> *The earth dries up and withers, the world languishes and withers; the heavens languish together with the earth. The earth lies polluted under its inhabitants; for they have transgressed laws, violated the statutes, broken the everlasting covenant. Therefore, a curse devours the earth, and its inhabitants suffer for their guilt; therefore, the inhabitants of the earth dwindled, and few people are left. (Isa 24:4–6)*

Here, the world is far from its original intent where judgment has now been brought upon it because the people have violated an everlasting covenant. It behooves us not to repeat or be in jeopardy of repeating a violation of the everlasting covenant. But as we return to the ground, let us gain a greater sensitivity toward creation and participate in the wearing of each other.

As We Return to The Ground: Let Us Wear Each Other

Ellen Davis in *Scripture, Culture, and Agriculture* asserts that Leviticus is "a theologically profound vision of the complexity and interdependence of the created order, and grapples with the difficult question of how humans may responsibly participate in that order." Yet Davis states that there is a widespread Christian disregard for Leviticus. This might give the impression that it has less urgency or relevance than other books of the Bible. Leviticus—Hebrew: *torat kohanim* or the Priest's Manual (Instruction)—might be viewed as instruction for the "priests" only, but it is a book for all of us. Davis's scholarly approach names Leviticus as the "profound connection between humans and land—specifically, arable land, the proximate source of all plant and animal life. Leviticus views land as a complex material reality fraught with religious and spiritual significance." For this examination, Davis's continued thought is of most importance: "Land was the means of subsistence for nearly every Israelite and thus could also be seen as a mirror of human existence, an extended sanctuary, and a partner in covenant and agent of covenant justice." Therefore, to be good stewards of the land is to fix the way one sees oneself in relation to it—in covenant relationship.

Davis in *Preaching the Luminous Word* describes royal priesthood as *wearing each other before God.* Davis expounds on how Aaron, Israel's first high priest, "wore the breastplate of judgment into the sanctuary—all goldwork, and studded with twelve great jewels, each engraved with the name of one of the tribes of Israel." Aaron, literally, wore the tribes of Israel over his heart into God's presence. Merriam-Webster defines *wear* as "to bear . . . to carry on the person," or "to hold the rank, dignity, or position signified by an ornament." Likewise, I extend the thought of *wearing each other*—where there is no separation between us—as creatures of God's creation: carrying, caring, and holding the dignity of one another unto life and death so that no harm is done to the other; but beautification and holiness unto the heavens. However, *wearing each other*, for some, may be burdensome because the wearing may signify a dependence on or an interdependence and the need for responsibility. Therefore, the concept may be rejected.

But moreover, Davis teaches that the "goal of Leviticus is that Israel should live out its Sinai-based vocation to be a holy people" (Exod 19:6). Leviticus speaks to those who are striving to be God's holy people. The Black Church seeks to live out what it means to be God's holy people. Its rituals—communion, weddings, funerals, etc.—are the protocols for reverential acts with communal involvement that provide ways to deal with sin and death. As members of the Black Church, we practice rituals and hold them sacred. Moreover, we believe that our covenant relationship with God is strengthened through the execution, implementation, and embodiment of ritual. Not only is there a call to ritual but a call to the ground in foundational holiness and purification in lifestyle, in being, and in becoming.

A fundamental characteristic of God is holiness, which all of God's people should seek to embody. Israel Knohl in *The Sanctuary of Silence* notices the unique covenant built on the intimacy and the closeness that God has with Israel. Knohl suggests that God is near to creation and looks over it, and that our obedience to God's *holy code* comes with benefits and our violations of it come with punishments. From holiness comes righteousness, and from righteousness comes justice (criminal, social, psychological, or environmental). Israel became idolatrous and not single-minded. Israel forgot that they were God's possession. Following this investigation, it is safe to say that we are not to be polluters of this world, and we risk becoming idolatrous when our attention is distracted from what is central—God. Specifically, let us not be defilers of land with the placement of toxic chemicals. Expounding on Leviticus 18:28, Davis declares that the land has a moral sensitivity—an agency of a land that vomits out its defilers. Davis asserts "that the land cares how we use or misuse it." Holiness extends itself to the ground where the Black Church can benefit from a "sensitivity that perceives land a living being."

There is mystery in the ground—the fertile soil. Yet, God is calling us to it and to find the glory that is inevitably attached to it and therefore to us. Davis states that "from a *deep green* perspective of Leviticus, land is an active participant in covenantal living." Leviticus 25:23 tells us that "the land shall not be sold in perpetuity (beyond reclaim), for the land is mine [the Lord's]; with me you are but aliens and tenants." Our grounding should be cemented only in covenantal relationship and not in possession. God calls us to "lie down in green pastures" (Ps 23: 2), and to "lie down in peace and to not be afraid" (Lev 26:6). Yet, when we use harmful chemicals in burial, we threaten turning these "green pastures" into toxic graveyards and thus preventing the possibility of lying down in peace. These "lie down" statements can apply not only to our life but also to our death, when we are returned to the soil by cremation, burial, or exposure. God is calling us to the ground—to God's pastures, the fields, the earth, to be meek and lowly—to reclaim foundational principles and theologies that are natural and of nature and embrace our creaturely status. Also, God promises to raise us up again. Thus, there is no need to put *money in the ground*—silver and gold—for we shall be raised in the glory of the Lord. This is beautiful!

As we are called to the ground—literally and figuratively—let us not be distracted by the "flashy" but remember that living within our limits is comely and beautiful, says Davis. With this agrarian reading of Leviticus—one that reads with a culture of preservation and care of the land at its heart—our hope is to acquire the beauty and the blessing that resides in the materials of creation.

Certainly, there rests a beauty in honoring covenantal relationships. Davis argues that when we open our eyes to see, at times, there is a pain; yet the experience of seeing is always accompanied by surprise. Seeing with God and with God's original intent brings about a wholesomeness and a healthiness that is indeed beautiful. Failure to see and obey, to guard and to live into holy awareness comes at a cost, a separation from God (see Lev 26:19–20 on disobedience). As I extend the argument to funeral practices: How might sowing our seeds "in vain" relate to burying money in fancy coffins? How might poisonous burial practices make the "earth like copper" and the lands infertile (Lev 26:19–20)? "Know ye not that your body is the temple of the Holy Ghost which is in you, which ye have of God, and ye are not your own? For ye are bought with a price: therefore, glorify God in your body, and in your spirit, which are God's" (1 Cor 6:19–20 KJV). Here is a theology of the body—the body as a temple or a tomb. Might our disobedience toward the things of God cost or cause separation from, or space between, us and God? God cannot and will not abide in a polluted temple. Again, the fruitful yet fragile beauty of the fertile earth constitutes an ongoing call of responsibility and repentance, and for a change of life.

As we return to the ground, are we, in essence, denying our beauty or dustiness by prolonging the decaying process? But let us wear each other continually, as Davis proclaims, "so that heaven may be more beautiful." So, therefore, taking on the Levitical priestly posture to lead; and not to be (as Brueggemann describes) "robbed of the courage and power to think an alternative thought," but as 1 Peter 2:9 proclaims, for the royal priesthood to come into the marvelous light.

The Doctrine of Creation: Attentiveness to Our Creation and Aesthetics

Colin Gunton in *The Doctrine of Creation* suggests that it is time to reconsider the doctrine of creation. One reason for reconsidering, Gunton argues, is to gain a clarifying view of *in the beginning*, and he focuses on human action in and toward the world. Willie Jennings asserts that to gain a healthy and mature doctrine of creation, one must have a deep sense of connectivity—one not simply rooted in domination. We must embody an understanding of priesthood in which we lead in the things of God and are co-creatures with other creatures. In her exploration of Genesis 1, Davis boldly asserts that "there is no extensive exploration of the relationship between God and humanity that does not factor the land and its fertility into that relationship." If this is so, it is in keeping with the covenant God made with the land. Genesis 9:13 clearly states that God is not only in covenant with Noah but is in covenant with earth: "I have set my bow in the clouds, and it shall be a sign of the covenant between me and the earth." Davis speaks to Genesis as housing God's everlasting covenant with Noah and the earth, the fertile soil. This fertile soil is potent ground ripe for gestation, preservation, and reproduction. In other words, the soil is healthy—ripe for something to happen, for birthing, and a move of God. Soil is a complex web of relationships that represents a deeply mysterious bridge, says Norman Wirzba in *Thanks for the Dirt*. Therefore, Wirzba contends, soil is sacred and holy. Because of the convincing arguments of scholars like Wirzba and Davis, churches should educate families about funeral practices that are minimally injurious to the earth and insist that the funeral industry adopt and advance such practices.

Additionally, there exists a theme of goodness in Genesis: "God saw everything he had made, and indeed it was very good" (1:31). Goodness is extended to the production of that which is good—"be fruitful and multiply" (1:28). As Davis skillfully ties creation and goodness to beauty by teaching us that the fruitfulness is a fragile beauty that constitutes an ongoing call to responsibility and repentance, the concept or ideology of the fragile beauty is worth weighing inside of the Black church funeral practices toward our response to the goodness of God.

In Genesis 2, we witness the attentiveness of God toward creation in the placement of Adam in the garden—an indication of blessings, goodness, beauty, and paradise. According to Davis, the relationship of the word Adam to *adamah* shows how closely related humans are to the fertile soil (or our "dustiness"). This further bridges the inseparability of God, land,

and people with blessings for creation: rain, fertility, and harvest. Yet, with blessings and placement comes an expectation of covenantal loyalty. But Davis makes a critical point of divine intentions with a wider view of placement and having dominion as one "of *skilled mastery* that represents God and God's interest where God intends humans, other creatures and the land itself to flourish." But when dominion goes wrong, as seen in the flood narrative in Genesis 6, God has to step in showing what loyalty look like (Genesis 9).

Based on these scholarly reviews, I ask the question, "Are our practices in line with God's goodness and love toward creation?" Certainly, we do not want our sowing of God's seed to be in vain, or our practices to make the earth like copper and infertile lands (Lev 26:19–20). Today, might God be dissatisfied with our treatment of, or lack of attentiveness toward, creation and our handling or harming of the ground and environment?

The True Nature of Beauty: A Strong Covenantal Relationship is Christian Beauty

Bishop Ambrose of Milan (c. 339–397) can assist the Black church and its community in adjusting its aesthetic of beauty—its views and behaviors—regarding funerals toward an alternative aesthetic of beauty. Bishop Ambrose, largely known for his role in converting Saint Augustine to Christianity and maybe less known for his treatise *On the Duties of the Clergy*, which is relevant here, was an important figure in the early church. Regarding his death, he instructed ecclesial leaders to guide God's people to "Put off, O Jerusalem, the garment of thy mourning and affliction, and clothe thyself in *beauty*, the glory which God hath given thee forever." For the Church, its ecclesial leadership and community, this is a message that needs affirmation.

I emphasize three elements of Ambrose's thought that can be helpful to Black churches in embracing a stronger ecological theology related to funeral practices. First, Ambrose affirms "the beauty of the perishable body, which will come to an end with sickness or old age but the reputation for good deserts, subject to no accidents and never to perish." Ambrose continues: "you, too, have indeed your own beauty, furnished by the comeliness of virtue, not of the body, to which age puts not an end, which death cannot take away, nor any sickness injure. Let God alone be sought as the judge of loveliness, who loves even in less beautiful bodies the more beautiful souls." Ambrose takes our sight off the perishable or the corruptible and places it on the incorruptible. In other words, it is not material beauty that constitutes true beauty, but the goodness of souls, which outlive worldly trappings.

So too, Black churches are obligated to put off the old garment of not considering or prioritizing creation and at the time of death, clothe itself in the beauty, the glory of creation which God has already graciously given. But how does what Ambrose believes shape what we might think about death in the Church? I argue that this pursuit of perfection or beauty extends even into death and funeral processing. Dr Betty Holley would suggest that the Church has largely been silent on climate change and environmental degradation and has not, at the very least, formed a united voice toward ways to reduce its negative ecological footprint. Likewise, the Black Church should create space and form a collective voice toward an ecological theology regarding death care.

Second, Ambrose extends Plato's thought of wisdom of the flesh to wisdom from God. Wisdom and virtue bind the whole city, the Republic, (the soul) together. For Plato, wisdom is to know the good. For Ambrose, wisdom is devotion and reverence to God as the Supreme good, the good bound to Abraham and the God of Abraham, the good bound in the covenant relationship of God, land, and people. If God says it is good and prudent, must we the Church not see it as such? Advocating for the care of the earth, the holy usage of and engagement with the land, is the kind of perfection that a bereavement ministry seeks with funeral processing. Ambrose would suggest for the Church not to pollute the mind but to be healthy in the soul.

Thirdly, for Ambrose, wisdom is to justice as faith is to piety—there is not one without the other. Relatedly, there is no separation of wisdom and justice—just one form of virtue divided up. God is the source of all things, so we never own anything. In the Black Church, our highest piety is to God and not to our parental and other relationships. Ambrose suggests that piety, which includes modesty and decorum, reveals the integrity of the life of the inner person and the action of the outer person reveals something about their character. Ambrose is concerned about clergy taking on a certain persona of affectation or something that is not real. For Ambrose, to see beauty in one's authentic self, in modesty and purity, is to prove what is the good, acceptable, and the perfect will of God. Ambrose would suggest that modesty is what we all should have versus an arrogance where one points to oneself even as one witness of God: I must decrease that God might increase. Might these thoughts extend to creation and our behaviors toward the environment? Faith in God becomes the priority to our leadership, Ambrose would tell us. If God is the supreme being, then we have absolute dependence on God in life and even more so in death.

At the time of death and funeral processing, the Church must perfect its hope in God, accepting that "to dust you shall return" (Gen 3:19), and that there is no separation of what is mortal from what is dust. As we return to the dust, let us perfect the ways in which we care for the earth and ensure that we are not polluting our return and the source of our future sustenance. We are to take care of what God has gifted us. We must return to the earth in the most life-giving of ways—fulfilling God's purpose for creation. As we return to the dust and the earth an appropriate human response to the sacred is to allow the land to now feed from or be joined to us without barriers. Yet we live in bubbles—bubbles of control and comfort. But in doing so, we impact and shape ecological realities even if we are not aware of them, or we try to ignore them if we are aware. So, these bubbles are idolatrous creations that ignore the truth of our creatureliness, especially in relation to the rest of creation.

The Beauty of Creation Care

As stated previously, it is appropriate for Black churches to embody a theology of ecology where priesthood represents leadership in the things of God and acknowledges that we are co-creatures with other creatures. Community leaders and ecclesial leaders must direct us toward the care of creation and being better stewards of the land. Willie Jennings states that "we must first recognize that we are *possessed by* (belong to God), and so therefore, we have limited *possession of* what we claim as our own." With Jennings's foundational principles and other assertions by Davis, Knohl, Fox, and Brueggemann that our connectivity to the land is holy and covenantal, the *New Interpreter's Bible* guides the Church further into its place as a royal priesthood—its beauty, majesty, and splendor—as found in Isaiah 62:3; Deuteronomy 7:6, and 1 Peter 2:9, which says, "But ye are a chosen generation, a royal priesthood, a holy nation, a peculiar people; that ye should shew forth the praises of him who hath called you out of darkness into his marvelous light" (KJV).

The *New Interpreter's Bible* points us to Colossians where the inheritance of God's people moves beyond the terrestrial and into the transcendent realm of light. Light has connotations of transcendent splendor, the environment of the heavenly world, and of holiness and ethical purity, as seen in Colossians 1:12–14, which says "giving thanks to the Father, who has enabled you to share in the inheritance of the saints in the light. He has rescued us from the power of darkness and transferred us into the kingdom of his beloved Son, in whom we have redemption, the forgiveness of sins." We are enthroned—sharing in the inheritance—by God's divine power. This enthronement invokes the show of divine love to others—especially the marginalized—the least, the lonely, and the left out. For the church to embody our royal priesthood, we must see all creation as part of our concern and care. We are in the midst of God's majesty and splendor: the grass of the fields and the flowers of the trees. We must be attentive to the state of the wind, the sea, and the rocks; and what they teach us. The majesty and splendor of God is continual and never ceases or fails. For many, the natural world might not appear to be great or of much value. However, the church is called to join the psalmist in affirming that "the earth is the Lord's, and the fullness there of" (Psalm 24:1 KJV). Let the glory of the Lord rise among us. Let us be transformed and engaged in the metamorphic beauty of God.

Creation Care: Peace, Shalom, and Wellbeing

It is in the best interest of the Black Church to practice eco-theological awareness for convergence, community, honoring our covenantal relationship, and simply, for peace—not only to live in peace but also to live a transformative life that is life-changing and life-giving. Unfortunately, as Fred Bahnson shares in *Soil and Sacrament*, "We have tilled the *adamah* but have not kept it." In death we have too often poisoned the soil; or at minimum, failed to allow the soil to eat, to feast, and to live from us. As we return to the soil, the church has the opportunity to foster peace and beauty inside of the death and funeral processing.

This book seeks not only to raise awareness about the toxic consequences of traditional funeral practices, but also to point the Black Church toward an ecological theology with a true essence of beauty and a "life that is healthful." Wisdom is the ability to discern God's righteous order—life-giving designs—and to teach communities how to act in conformity with that order. Helping the Black Church to embody the truth that "life created in God's image is meant to confirm other forms of life, into a single harmonious order." This behavior brings about a wellness of soul that is sustainable, eternal, and indeed, beautiful.

Black Church ecclesial leaders cannot discard the responsibility of first embodying then leading ecological faith toward creation care and strengthening our covenant relationship with God. I urge them to "let there be no separation between you and the dust of the ground." I am encouraging the "priests" to take their rightful places (postures) and to lead in this crucial area. While churches generally focus on life through salvation of a person's soul and with fellowship and the eating of natural food, they are more challenged by the experience of death—and when death occurs, the church is often silent about its (covenantal) responsibility to the environment. Often, Black churches send families to funeral homes that have historically added to the commercialization of the industry and shown little to no regard for the use of toxins and the impact of those toxins on living bodies and organisms, including the land. The church, then, is negligent in its efforts to help members gain an ecological faith, especially in death. But in death, Black church leaders can embody what it means to be the church in the most life-giving of ways, even in funeral preparation and processing. If this is achieved, Black churches could solidify their partnership in global sustainability and live out the covenantal relationship between God, God's people, and the land. This would be holy. Indeed, this would be beautiful, and certainly this would be a *glad funeral.*

As we turn to the next chapter, we explore green funeral practices in an effort to offer the Black Church a new aesthetic regarding its approach to death as a part of increasing its ecological faith and awareness. Ultimately, my desire is to help Black churches embrace an ecological theology regarding funeral practices and to be better stewards of the earth, strengthen their covenantal relationship, and conduct ministry in the most life-giving of ways, which is indeed beautiful. But what challenges does the green funeral pose for Black churches?

4

The Green Funeral

Even with its challenges and controversies, North Carolina Black Church funerals are important and should be an enduring practice. I propose that there is a more excellent way for the Black Church to engage families in the preparation of death by connecting the spiritual with the practical to best honor our relationship with God, the earth, and each other. There is a more excellent way for the Black Church to determine how best to incorporate dying into living, to experience death as a part of life, and to reclaim agency—a directness or closeness—in funeral processing. How best do we infuse human experience back into death in the most life-giving of ways? I propose that the Black Church's participation in greener funeral options as opposed to modern traditional practices gives us the chance to remedy, or reconcile, our modern disconnection—whether perceived or actual—with death, and much more. I offer a new approach to the Black Church funeral, the green funeral. Green funerals are one way for Black Christian leaders to embody creation care. By promoting more environmentally friendly funeral practices,

Christian leaders can better serve God, God's people, and the land.

What Is a Green Funeral?

Suzanne Kelly in *Greening Death* suggests that, in many ways, the green burial is about a return to the past. Native Americans have engaged in cremations and natural burials—wrapping the body in a blanket and burying directly in the ground. And although impeded by modern cemeteries, Muslim and Jewish laws have never totally relinquished natural burial principles and practices. Recent publications regarding green burials acknowledge Ramsey Creek Preserve in Westminster, South Carolina (founded in 1996) as the "first green or natural, burial ground (cemetery) in the United States."

Lee Webster, of the Green Burial Council (GBC), states that "a green funeral is a general term and commonly used to describe post-death care, from death to disposition which uses only natural means. A green burial allows full interment into the ground in a manner that does not inhibit decomposition. This requires use of nontoxic preservation techniques and organic materials with minimal carbon footprints. The three top defining characteristics of any green burial are: absence of vault, non-toxic preparation of the body, and use of containers made of organic materials." Embracing and encouraging green funerals is a critical contemporary contribution for Black churches to practice a holistic faith that helps to liberate the environment from toxins.

Although Kelly lists the top reasons why people choose to *green* death as: "1. minimizing impact on the environment, 2. back to old tradition, 3. cost, 4. spiritual or religious reasons; and finally, 5. having a do-it-yourself ethic," she suggests that choosing to green death aids in restoring our tie to the earth—with closeness and without borders or barriers. The purpose of the green burial is to strengthen our connection and relationship not only to each other but also to the environment and to the earth. I extend the purpose of the green burial to the funeral to ultimately strengthen our covenant relationship with God.

The green funeral is a nontoxic approach to post-death care. It considers all creation and creates sacred and communal opportunities toward participation. In other words, the green funeral is intentional about keeping The Creator in matters that involve creation by inviting ecclesial or church participation. In addition, the green funeral treasures family and community, and therefore, is for all people.

The GBC promotes "a green burial [as] a way of caring for the dead with minimal environmental impact that aids in the conservation of natural resources, reduction of carbon emissions, protection of worker health, and the restoration and/or preservation of habitat." In addition, Lee Webster of the GBC states that "a green funeral is commonly used to describe post-death care, from death to disposition which uses only natural means," Here, *The Green Funeral* expands these definitions to include the sacred and communal.

While *The Green Funeral* holds true to the GBC concepts, it extends the thoughts of those considering participation toward a more theological, inclusive, and diversified methodology, one that is based in relationship with God, people, and land. God is in covenant with Godself, people, and land; so therefore, we should be as well. While hard to believe, one can be an environmentalist, combating climate change and aid in global sustainability efforts, yet not be for all people. *The Green Funeral* can assist. Where relationships are present, *The Green Funeral* seeks to strengthen what already exists.

The Green Funeral invites the church to participate in efforts to strengthen its covenant with God, land, and people. So, to extend the concept of a funeral is nothing new. But a green funeral best supports natural or greening death in this present age. It is presented here specifically as an introduction for some and presented to others as being for all people.

In addition, *The Green Funeral*, like practices in many cultures, including Native American and African American cultures, broadens the concept of funeral to run beyond the four walls of a traditional church service and what happens with the body—the initial handling, preparation and deposition—to include community. Often, prior to the traditional church services, visitation is held at the home of the deceased. People flood the streets and the home, sharing stories, eating food, and listening to music. Then after the funeral services and deposition, the joining continues with additional fellowship and food, in what is called the repass. In the Black community, when one goes to a funeral, *the going* may include any or all the aforementioned. Funerals are sacred. Funerals are communal. Therefore, *The Green Funeral* invites one to think and rethink, consider and reconsider, family participation. What, if any, are the local and state laws governing family involvement? Who can transport and prepare the body? To what extent does the family desire to participate? And, of course, who owns the land and how might more people have access to a green funeral?

It matters what we put in the ground. Kelly remembers environmental activists Rachel Carson and Aldo Leopold who, in the United States, gave voice to the harm done to nature and the need for a healthier earth. In addition, Kelly recalls the 2010 *New York Times* article that read: "At the end of an eco-conscious life, there is a final choice a person can make to limit his or her impact on the planet: a green funeral." As Americans become more eco-conscious in life, this consciousness must also include all things related to death. The Black church should be no different. Is not death a part of living? *Going green* is often used to describe businesses that reduce toxins in food or in the air, and the general decrease of other harmful environmental factors associated with everyday living. But, what about in death? *The International Journal of Environmental Research and Public Health* illuminates its concern regarding burials and soil contamination, noting that "burial loads have a direct impact on soil-mineral content and thus cemeteries can be regarded as anthropogenic sources of contamination." This contamination could possibly come from the deceased's body, preservatives in the wooden casket, and the paints and material used for handles or other adornments chosen to "enhance" the appearance or the aesthetics of the casket. Ultimately, this study is concerned with the potential health risks associated with the leaching of all harmful minerals into the groundwater. The green burial considers the same types of factors in death and burial that one would consider in life.

Kelly upholds the GBC as the "standard bearer of green burial terrain, identifying and certifying burial grounds." According to the Green Burial Council, a green burial "necessitates the use of non-toxic and biodegradable materials, such as caskets, shrouds, and urns." The Council (and this book) is not labeling any end-of-life ritual as wrong but "advocates for green services and products that help to minimize the environmental impact of last acts."

Green Funeral Components

In addition to my extended definition of the green funeral where I not only frame the green funeral as a general term meaning "from death to disposition," as Lee Webster has defined it, but I make space for, and invite, Black ecclesial leaders to join in this ecological faith movement. From the

GBC, here are a few elements or considerations to help the Black Church rethink funerals:

1. Consider biodegradable coffins or the use of shrouds—All GBC approved caskets, urns and shrouds must be constructed from plant-derived, recycled plant-derived, natural, animal, or unfired earthen materials, including shell, liner, and adornments.
2. Stop the use of vaults—Although vaults are concrete and made from natural materials, the manufacturing of the materials and transporting of vaults uses a tremendous amount of energy and causes enormous carbon emission. In the United States, vault manufacturing requires the production of 1.6 tons of reinforced concrete. On the other hand, there exists concerns that surround thinner vaults.
3. Stop embalming—Specifically, stop using traditional formaldehyde embalming fluid. Formaldehyde has been shown to cause health issues for the embalmer and the possibility of soil contamination. Finally,
4. Rethink cremations—If sought, at least, use a crematory that considers reduced emissions.

In greening death, I acknowledge the importance of meeting people where they are. However, I emphasize the criticalness of keeping one's eye on the larger global sustainability picture and ultimately on the care of creation.

Green Funeral and Traditional Black Funeral Comparisons and Contrasts

The green funeral is an alternative approach to the traditional and toxic Black Church funeral. In its attempt to further explain and educate the public on green burials, the GBC recognizes standards (or levels) of cemetery certification: conservation, natural, and hybrid. Conservation certification—which may broadly take into consideration preservation and restoration—is the highest standard and includes a "guarantee preservation of the burial ground by deed restriction, conservation easement, or other legally binding and irrevocable agreement that runs with the land and is enforceable in perpetuity;" an ecological impact assessment starting with "a property baseline document that includes existing ecological conditions and sensitive area analysis which is updated periodically to assess future property/habitat conditions and plant inventory"; and the development of a maintenance and operations manual which is used by "all staff, contractors, and volunteers to implement site goals, policies, and best practices." A natural burial ground is less restrictive yet must conduct an ecological impact assessment. Then, the least restrictive—hybrid cemeteries—must develop and maintain usage of a maintenance and operations manual. For the larger audience of people considering greening death, there are variations not only between these categories but inside of each category.

I agree with the concept of *levels of greening* because it is indicative of the fact that there is not a one-size-fits-all approach that fully encompasses the needs of every family. Greening methods may range from family members washing and wrapping the body in cloth (or a simple wood box) and directly lowering it into the ground, as seen in the Jewish and Muslims cultures; to a sky burial as seen in the Tibetan culture in which the dead are "dismembered and left on mountaintops to be feasted upon by vultures." Yet for the Western world, a green funeral may consist of any of these levels of greening.

Since funeral rites and rituals are of great importance to Black churches and where funerals, for most spiritual and practical purposes, have resisted adaptation and change, what might this reclaiming resemble? Although we might not be quite ready to go back to bathing, dressing, and sheltering the deceased to lie in repose in the front rooms of our homes, many Black Church funeral practices have remained unchallenged as profitability in the funeral industry has increased. A green funeral may consist of any of the following variations:

1. Green Burial A direct burial is the depositing of a body into the earth without separation or division of body-to-earth or with the possible usage of biodegradable earth friendly materials. Direct burial is recognized by the GBC as the most natural approach to greening death. It excludes vaults, headstones, and other chemical or non-biodegradable materials. Heidi Hannapel of Bluestem Cemetery asserts in a Zoom conversation that "natural burial [or green burial] is still considered the most ecologically friendly" burial option.

2. Cremation The number of cremations in the United States is rising, and according to Hannapel, many people think of cremation as an eco-friendly option but it does release carbon dioxide into the air. Cremation is "the process of reducing the body of the deceased to bone fragments, sodium and calcium phosphate, and ashes by the use of high heat incineration by fire; the creation of an average body uses enough natural gas and electricity to produce 140 pounds of CO_2." Admittedly, I have known community neighbors who chose cremation because it is a less intrusive quick fix—it has the lowest economic impact and is not drawn out, where funeral services or a church is involved. However, one could have a funeral or church services in combination with cremation.

Cremation servicing often includes embalming for viewing and then cremation. Yet, a more excellent choice of death care for cremations is direct cremation, which involves no injection of chemicals into the body for viewing purposes and where the body goes directly into the crematory for cremation. But is the chosen crematory using the newest or most efficient machinery? An increased awareness of crematory machinery is recommended inside of greening death to aid in limiting the amount of carbon being placed in the air.

3. Refrigeration The GBC recognizes the use of refrigeration (or keeping the body on ice) to keep a deceased's body at a cold temperature and slow down decomposition. Refrigeration is used instead of embalming. However, refrigeration requires that funeral directors have the means to cool the body and to bury the body in a quicker fashion. The Cremation Association of America (CANA) asserts that "families should be provided with the option to [formally] view their loved one even if they don't want embalming." Refrigeration could be a key practice for viewing the body before either cremation or burial.

4. Human Composting (Recomposing) In the United States, human composting, or natural organic reduction (recompose) is gaining traction. Located outside of Seattle, the Recompose company is turning dead bodies into soil. Unlike cremation, no fire, carbon, nitrogen, heat, water, or oxygen is used. Recomposing takes two weeks to a month and generally costs $5,500 per body. Other states are looking into being providing recomposing services in their areas.

5. Human Aquamation (Resomation) Elisabeth Keijzer in "Environmental Impact of Different Funeral Technologies" concludes that resomation has the least impact on the environment compared to traditional burial and cremation. The alkaline hydrolysis process uses natural elements of 95 percent water (heated), 5 percent alkali solution of potassium hydroxide (KOH), and sodium to break down the deceased's body into just bones. Aquamation is being used in the disposal of bodies donated to science, and only uses 10 percent of the energy of a traditional cremation and produces no air emissions like traditional cremations. Clay-Barnette Funeral Home and Aquamation Center, the first funeral home in North Carolina to provide the process of alkaline hydrolysis, advertises that "while most charge on average $2,200-$3,500 for cremation, our local aquamation charge starts at $1,995." Recently, the process of aquamation made headline news with the death and ecological funeral of anti-apartheid leader and Anglican archbishop emeritus Bishop Desmond Tutu. As a sign of being a champion for the environment, during the funeral, Bishop Tutu's body rested in a simple pine coffin; thereafter, entered the aquamation process then interred at St. George's Cathedral in Cape Town. Bishop Tutu's example is worthy of us all to follow.

6. A Hybrid Approach As stated earlier, there are various levels of awareness or involvement in greening death, from managing the deceased's body to the related funeral practices. The ecclesial leader can become part of the greening death movement. Doing so will help equip the leaders to lead families to consider greening death prior to and during the process of dying and make this pastoral leadership more credible. For leaders to take this step, I present possible opportunities for the Black Church to build ecological faith throughout the entirety of one's life. I show how an ecological theological framework leads families to honor the dead more nobly through practicing responsible financial and environmental stewardship.

With the onset of new deathcare trends the GBC is challenged as to which process to endorse and is in the process of having further discussions regarding better ecological death processing. Unlike traditional or mainstream offerings, a hybrid approach to deathcare displays a heightened awareness of global sustainability efforts and allows the family to incorporate unique levels, minimum or maximum, based on comfort level, availability, and accessibility. Yet, an effort has been made and consideration has been given toward the greater efforts of greening. For some, a hybrid approach may be considered as a middle ground or a step toward greening death or obtaining a level of ecological faith, even in death, instead of none or making no advance at all.

The Green Funeral Is a Response to Environmentalism

The green funeral is a response to environmentalism, environmental theology, and creation care, helping to bridge gaps between science and spirituality. Merriam-Webster defines environmentalism as "advocacy of the preservation, restoration, or improvement of the natural environment." John Hart in *What Are They Saying About Environmental Theology?* extends this definition of environmentalism toward God. Hart offers an environmental theology that is concerned with "the intrinsic value of all creatures and earth, responsibility of the usage of earth's resources a sense of intergenerational responsibility and a heightened consciousness of the immanence of the Creator in creation." Douglas Moo in *Creation Care* describes creation care as "our ethical responsibility for the non-human world." Moo proclaims that creation care speaks to more than the care for creation but connotes a view of creation that grounds our care in how we think about creation that will govern how we care for it. Then, the Lausanne Movement simply states creation care this way: the stewardship of God's creation. The green funeral is not only a response to environmentalism, environmental theology, and creation care but also promotes ecological faith.

The Green Funeral Promotes Ecological Faith

As the Black Church looks for creative ways to embody ecological faith, the green funeral is an excellent way to engage.

The Advancement of Ecological Faith

According to BioExplorer.net's history of ecology, German philosopher Ernst Haeckel coined the term *ecology* in 1869. Ecology "comes from the Greek word *Oikos* meaning 'household' and *logos* meaning 'study of,' therefore the 'study of nature's household.' Relating this definition to science, ecology becomes the study of the management of the natural environment which includes the relations of organisms with one another and to their surroundings." When combined with faith, ecology takes on a spiritual perspective. From this, we obtain an understanding of ecological faith that is rooted in the Creator, creation, and a hope for all living things.

The green funeral promotes ecological faith in Black Church traditions. Members of the Black Church community, like Green The Church, embody ecological faith. Green The Church is a Black Church community that seeks the advancement of ecological faith by creating ecological pathways for ecclesial leaders to thrive in the face of societal and personal challenges. According to its website, Green The Church identifies itself as "the Environmental Organization of the Black Church" and "stands at the intersection of the Black Church and the environmental movement." It speaks of a *green theology* that emphasizes the duty of Christians to protect God's creation. Ecological faith also looks like Trinity United Church of Christ in Chicago, Illinois. Pastor Otis Moss III extends the argument toward liberation. Like James Cone in "Whose Earth Is It Anyway?" and Dianne Glave in "Black Environmental Liberation Theology", Moss proclaims that "care of the land is intimately tied to Black liberation." From the church's green rooftop to improving eating habits, Trinity seeks to free its congregation and community from the economic, social, and environmental woes by putting their hands in the same soil and engaging in multigenerational environmental projects.

Ecological Faith and the Green Funeral

Ecological faith is meaningful and of value to Black Church funeral traditions. Embodying ecological faith through green funeral practices demonstrates an expanded view of covenant that not only includes the created order but emphasizes that if covenant is with God, then humanity has a responsibility to steward in a way that honors covenant. Therefore, Davis in *Getting Involved with God* proclaims that reverence for the earth and reverence for God cannot be separated. The green funeral concept acknowledges what Davis calls the "fragile beauty of the fertile earth that constitutes an ongoing call to responsibility, and for many of us, repentance and a change of life." I extend this argument to a call to holiness. Davis in *Scripture, Culture, and Agriculture* states that the prophet Isaiah leads us to apply ourselves to the telling diagnosis of "they have violated an everlasting covenant" through our abuse of creation. The green funeral concept acknowledges this fact and helps to strengthen our covenant with God.

The Green Funeral and The Black Church Funeral Tradition

The green funeral takes honoring covenant and the Black Church funeral to a next level. With the green funeral, the Black Church ecclesial leader takes responsibility and is accountable for all of creation and to God. Green funerals provide families as well as the Black Church with rich, meaningful healing while furthering legitimate environmental and societal aims such as protecting worker health, reducing carbon emissions, conserving natural resources, and preserving native habitat. The Black Church has a responsibility to act, to remember what God remembers, and to love what God loves. God loves the land. Embodying ecological faith says that the Black Church is a good steward, remembering what God remembers; and that the Black Church has a heart for what God has a heart for, loving what God loves.

5

To Be a Mango Tree

PEOPLE WHO HAVE a high regard for death care have more than likely considered their own mortality. Yet, how do we invite younger people into the death care and green funeral conversation? Considering a *redesign* of death practices (away from the traditional colonial capitalist approach—an approach that keeps the body separate from a natural decomposition process) is desired and sought after by the green funeral. Since death is a part of life, it is best spoken of, respectfully, in a casual conversation—maybe on a walk in the park or as a garden is planted; or creatively, inside of a planned conversation—when stress levels are low and before death occurs. These are not only great times to express your desires but great ways to introduce death to a younger generation.

Black Top 5ive podcast producer and digital creator, James Wilson, advocates for green funerals. In 2023, Wilson requested to interview me regarding my writings on greening death. During the interview, Wilson shares how his care for creation started with his mother and grandmother Ruby, and his own concern for ecological justice. Now, as a young adult, Wilson continues the conversation with his children. As a former board member of the Green Burial Council and current member of a Green Burial Council Peer Forum on Facebook, I am pleasantly surprised when young Black and Brown people take an interest in death conversations, let alone, greening death. Young people thinking, talking, and taking green action, is an indicator of not only intuition and innovation, revolution and resolve, but how natural burials will never go out of style. It is an indicator of thought processes that are not toward harming or alarming as the nightly news would portray but an indicator of care, protecting, conserving, and loving.

It is my pleasure to share a transcript of my interview with James Wilson here.

James Wilson: I've been wanting to have this conversation for a very long time; . . . let's just jump right in. I searched the internet and found your article written a few years ago called "Black Churches and Green Funerals." This is a topic of conversation that my grandmother and I had often. I'm an advocate for the preservation of the natural world, and the environment. We don't see a lot of people of African descent discussing this topic in a major way. I watched a show one time and they spoke about how African American (Black) women were the original caretakers of the planet. So, to come across your articles on creation care, I thought it was not only fitting but a testament to have this conversation with a Black woman. How did you get started having conversations about death, or simply, death conversations?

Dawson: Within a year of graduating with my doctoral degree in engineering, I was diagnosed with cancer. I had two friends that had cancer. We walked through cancer together. They had children, and I had a child. No one wants to leave their children; however, cancer forced us to think about our mortality. One of my friends (Lynette) said "I'm going to be alright; just take care of my children." So, out of the three, I remain to tell the story. I live my life testifying and helping others to walk through death experiences as well. Fast forward a few months, then, I was a minister in a church where funerals were frequent. During that season, it was not odd to have two or three a week. The outlier was if we had a week without a funeral. Being that I was the assistant to the bereavement and visitation pastor, I was tasked to not only go to funerals at the church but to funerals within a fifty-mile radius for the immediate family of church members. There, my awareness of everything about funerals and burials increased.

At one point, I thought I was going to be a mortician, or at least an assistant. I have family members in the mortuary business. I'm often asked to assist. Last week, I assisted in doing some things, just a little bit in that field.

Wilson: In thirty-six years, I have never heard of a bereavement ministry. This is my first time really hearing about it; yet we know that when one goes through bereavement, that can be a very vulnerable time. The decisions that families have to make during those times are under a different type of pressure because the mind is undergoing so much with coming to terms with the loss of the loved-one, along with the emotional attachments. In your article, you talked about green funerals. Let me set the stage for green funerals, which are a natural way of burying the dead. Today, there appears to be several ways to bury (or deposit) remains. I'm familiar with a few: where they naturally compost the body wherein it is introduced back to the earth. Then, I've seen some other ways, but I find it interesting that you correlated natural burials, green burials with the Black Church because there's a lot of traditionalism in the Black Church rooted in eurocentrism. When it comes to burying our dead, many are apprehensive and shy away. What is one way or several ways that we can combat traditionalism in the Black Church to make our people in the congregation more receptive to the idea of burying naturally?

Dawson: Thank you so much for your question. So, let's back up and let's start with definitions. Traditionally when we think of funeral and burial, we think of church but one can bury someone where the church is not involved. With talk about the green burial an organization comes to mind called the Green Burial Council (GBC). They are the ones currently in the United States that oversee natural burials. They have coined the term *green burial*—which is a natural burial; they have defined standards and determine if your planned burial or funeral meets these (their) standards or definitions of green. Again, the Green Burial Council (GBC)—which for a short time, I was a part of but at a certain point in my dissertation work, I needed to step away so I could finish school—is a place of reference to get involved and interested in green burials. So, do your homework. The Green Burial Council's website is where you can find definitions and talk about all things green burial. A green burial is essentially a natural burial where one ensures no harm is done to anyone, not even, the environment or the land. Is it considered "green" if someone is embalmed? The GBC would say no, that is not "green" because it is not totally natural. Well, how about cremation? Somebody might say "well I'm going to forego burial altogether and simply do cremation." Well, what does the Green Burial Council have to say about that? They would say, "we prefer to not emit fumes into the air or into the environment. We prefer that at death to lay the natural body in the ground maybe with some type of covering: a sheet, a shroud but let's just simply lay the body in the ground." Yet, you wish to consider green, but you have cremation in mind. It is advised for you to visit the mortuary or crematory asking questions about the age of the machinery and to learn about the number of fumes or carbon emissions that will be placed in the air. Then there is Recompose. As a proper noun, I believe Recompose is in Seattle, Washington. They bring in bodies then place them in these tubes or combs. Then add other natural materials (compost material). Given this, the right environment helps promote the decay process. Then within twenty or thirty days, the body decomposes, faster than the traditional expected decomposition timeframe with the injection of the embalming chemical or the embalming fluid (formaldehyde). Then, the remains are given back to the family. So, let's talk about the church. As a minister, I consider death and the return to the ground and to the creator as holy. With the green funeral, I inextricably keep the sacredness in the service with a member of the church (a God representative), one who is accountable to the people and to the land and ultimately to God by reminding the people, in this sacred hour, of God and what God is doing in the earth.

Wilson: I want to stay right there with green burials before we get to green funerals because it's such an interesting fact as you speak about research, definitions, and the education of our people. I am an advocate for children. I write children's books and here listening to you, I see why there needs to be education even in our children's science classes of this; because we as humans have such or have developed such a need to feel as though our loved ones are preserved the way that we knew them, when they go into the ground. But these thoughts are disturbing the natural biological process that God created. I was watching a crime show where police agencies use body farms to help determine specifics of crime scenes and how long the body's been dead. They spoke of coving the body so to keep vultures from getting to it; they spoke of how body fluid may initially kill the grass that surrounds the body but what I found fascinating was that after the body decomposes and usually after a few seasons, the grass and the beauty, the flowers grow back thicker than ever before. They showed why this natural process is necessary. But going back to green burials, you cite something in your article about ecological justice and that's a term that I was unfamiliar with. What can we do to make our people understand why ecological justice is so important? From your standpoint, what can we do to make our people understand?

Dawson: Well, let's be honest and get straight to the heart of the matter: we don't like to talk about death, right? We don't discuss it. It would be most beneficial to talk about death beforehand, as we have opportunity because in that moment everything happens so fast, right? Then, the stages of grief happen, where you don't know how you're going to react to death when death occurs. Grief can come and go and happen over a period of time. There are ebbs and flows to grief. Your grief may be different than mine. This is why having the conversation about death is important beforehand. Likewise, ecological justice is a big topic but if we talk about it ahead of time, we can cover more ground than being in the moment when the mortician explains what you are paying for, yet we have no clue of what he's talking about and the larger implications. We simply say, "handle it," right? Then later we reflect saying, "I could have done it differently." Regarding ecological justice when it comes to burials, let's talk about the environment. Let's talk about the land. Who owns the land? Who are the owners of most of the land in America? [White people.] So, let's put ownership of land into conversation because land is still very valuable. Are people still fighting wars over land

and oil, these days? [yes] Why? because land is important. Biblically, in Leviticus 25, God says "I shall remember the land." Therefore, we [as Christians] shall remember the land. It's important for us as a people [as Christians] to remember the land and to not harm it for sure. But guess what, we could stop right there but we choose not to. We want to continue to what? To enrich the land and engage with the land in the most life giving of ways. We don't want to simply not harm the land but we want to give back and replenish it so it can flourish.

Everybody has heard of six feet under right but recently states like Virginia and Minnesota have lessened regulations that minimize grave depth. So, if a natural burial occurs, the body decomposes quicker with the oxygen and the vibrations from the air in the topsoil in contrast to being six feet down; yet remain deep enough to avoid smell and scavengers. When you think about green burials, think "per state." My writings increase awareness and hopefully dispel misconceptions. At death, we do not have to be injected with formaldehyde. Tradition says that you have to be embalmed but this is a misconception. It is most beneficial to go and ask the funeral director or mortician, "what means do you have of keeping the body?"—where you can see your loved one without all the beautification processing. Yet, most go along with tradition. Just know that we have a say in what goes on when our loved one gets to the funeral home. We don't know what we don't know. Now, know that you have a say.

Wilson: Recently, I watched something where a lady was talking about backyard burials, and how per state, you should investigate because you actually had the right where you can be buried on your property. However, she advocated for a green cemetery because, as you know, if you are buried on your property, whenever you sell the land, you know that your loved one would still be there. Again, I feel this conversation regarding natural burials and greening death, it's so fascinating and necessary because life depends on us. What I mean by that is: my mother talked about the conversations I had with my grandmother when I often expressed how we are more alive in death than we are in life. Because when we are well in our physical bodies, we take from the environment more than we give back. We walk and talk and use a lot of water; we breathe the air, we're using the animals, and so forth. But in death, we can best give back and replenish the earth. In death, we are actually still serving a purpose of refeeding and refueling and replenishing, like you said, to enrich the soil. There are so many different connections to the natural elements that we can, in death, take advantage of: the ground and the air, even our bones. Our bones provide nutrients to the grown and other life sources and so forth. There is so much good we can do with natural burials; on the contrary, the thing about conventional burials I found is that it's almost like a legal form of pollution. In your article you cite many different things, you said we use almost 830,000 gallons of embalming fluid a year on burials and 97.5 tons of steel; and you cited so many different other things, but these things are harming the planet. For me, it's not only that but continuing to form a tradition where we are harming the planet. How do we get people to see that? Especially I find that the Black Church, who [kind of] sets the tone for the Black community because that's where you have many Black people gathering once a week; yet how can the Black Church reset the tone and inform our people about the pollution that's happening? Because again, this is a vulnerable time for families, but we must know when we owe it to one another to know the ramifications that this has on the planet, and on our future. So, as a minister, what can we do to get the Black Church to help the congregation and transcend this conversation onto our community to understand the harm that goes on through conventional burial?

Dawson: Yes, there are many sensitive topics in our land; and we're talking about one such topic today. My recommendation is to teach first; not to preach first. In ministry when approaching a difficult topic, it's good to maybe have a Bible study regarding the sensitive topic. It may be good to have a specific time set aside to talk about it before you get up and do a sermon on it. It's good to sit down and have a conversation. So, as you begin talking about it, you increase congregational awareness of what's going on. Again, that's what my writings are about; if you don't know what is happening, if you don't know that you can be buried *a different way*, then the church can assist.

Ecclesial leaders can be a big part of continued education by simply being aware of what is going on inside of funerals outside of your four walls; and what are you advocating for when the mortician and the other funeral directors come. What buy-in from the church is given? Church leader, what are you buying into, [let's say] for the funeral home staff that have been exposed to harmful chemicals. For the mortician or embalmer, whom the church works with and knows closely, it is recommended for that person to wear a mask during embalming and to put on protective gear (personal protection equipment, PPE). Additionally, there are stakeholders in the green burial and economic ramifications. Who are the stakeholders? (1) the green burial council—the ones who advocate, (2) the morticians and embalmers who get paid to do this work where costs reach into the thousands of dollars, (3) your loved one and family incurring the costs, and (4) the church and the community. Together we have allowed for the slowdown of the decomposition process. We beautify the body with lipstick and formaldehyde. While history reveals the close connection between mortician and the minister, today we do not diminish the value of the mortician to the community. But we [the community and church] take pride in our funeral homes. Often, the Black mortician is a minister in the local church since white morticians did not want to care for Black bodies. The Black mortician stepped up and stepped in. Today the Black mortician does not readily speak on green burials. To what extent has culture and tradition dictated how we conduct business today? I have even experienced a little pushback acknowledging that the current injection fluid (formaldehyde) is effective and works on the deceased body as desired. Because the funeral home industry seeks to deliver a good product, it may be understandable why change is hard. Given new products that exclude formaldehyde, that product is not readily desired or used. To what extent must we ensure that disease is not carried or spread with the body? At the early days of COVID, it was unclear if bodies carried disease or not. I'm talking about just in COVID times, but I believe there's a statute where morticians must ensure that they're not carrying disease through dead bodies. Apparently, there is a feeling of safety or protection with the current state instead of seeking to do something different with another non-toxic solution.

Wilson: I've heard these concerns or sentiments expressed where it is believed that people are worried about the spread of disease through a deceased body. I believe the chances of this are very low. As far as natural burial being toxic to the ground, professionally, I treat water for a living and becoming certified to treat the water we undergo testing of many types of bacteria and disease; more than what a dead body could give off. Modern day water filtration systems are designed with disinfectant to filter these things out. Most places in America, the primary water source is the river. We can only imagine what's in the river—something dead; it could be anything. Having concerns over the spread of disease are low. That is why I try to have conversations. When I do have these conversations, I try to get them to understand what [positive] impact a dead body could have [on the environment] and the carrying of a disease should really be the least of their concerns. But the overall impact to the ground into the natural world should be of one's concern because it is when we are gone when [our greatest] impact can begin. Yet going back to those statistics that you cited [in your article], just if you think about the millions of people who are embalmed, clothed, then put into a casket lined with fabric and made of metal which is not biodegradable, put into a vault and then put into the ground, the ecosystems that that disturbs and depletes is going to have far more negative ramifications than you know. Again, thinking and being concerned with the idea of a dead body carrying disease, the likelihood of that happening is extremely low.

Yet, going back to when you mentioned culture and the things that tend to win our buy-in. Let us speak more about the Bible studies to get buy-in from our church and community. I think Bible studies on this topic would be very effective. I grew up in the Christian Methodist Episcopal (CME) in Nashville (shout out to Phillips Chapel in Nashville, Tennessee). But my grandmother used to take us to another church. It was an African Methodist Episcopal (AME) church that had Vacation Bible school where the Bible was taught but also it was a chance to [kind of] reinforce other skill sets and our knowledge base around other subject matters. We talked a little bit about science, we read and did a little bit of math. So, now to consider having church conversations geared toward the young regarding greening (sustainability, greening death and death care), I think that would be very effective, as you stated, to inform our people and normalize the concept of natural burials and the obligation we have as ecological justice advocates.

In your article, you cited a verse from Isaiah 20 verses four and five: "The earth dries up and withers; the world languishes and withers; the heavens anguish together with the earth. The earth lies polluted under its inhabitants, for they have transgressed laws, violated the statutes, broken the ever-lasting covenant." Can you talk about the covenant that we have with God and the earth? Can you expound upon that? I just want to hear from a minister's perspective.

Dawson: Well, hold me to the idea of a covenant. But please allow me to back-track. (Which may very well lead into a covenant conversation.) Because when you talked about the church, let's talk about church leaders because ecclesial leaders and ministers must be held accountable, to educate oneself. When you get into a certain just say a career path when you say this is my destination even as a minister you have to continue to educate yourself, read articles, read what's going on in the land today; not just read your Bible but you have to read about what's going on in the world and in the land so that's what my writings are about: to increase this awareness and to be knowledgeable of what you speak. I'm saying to the leaders, again when we mentioned Bible Study but let's talk about funerals in our church (Lesson Learned) and what I have done or what we had in a certain church. I want to do a "shout-out" to Russell CME Church but now I'm at Saint Joseph AME Church also in Durham, North Carolina. But let's talk lessons learned. When you conduct or do something in your church, go back and talk about it. Likewise, we'll need to talk about funerals. Some would say, "we've been doing this forever and there is nothing we can learn, there is nothing that we need to improve on." But there is always room for improvement. There are always creative ways for growth. So, let's talk about funerals and the stakeholders. Let's talk about the obituaries and what signs and signals we are giving the congregants with what is said inside of the obituaries. Let's talk about a new thing where the morticians conduct what is called the Final Walk, when they take the casket out let's talk about that and what does that represent.

(So, covenant.) My dissertation speaks to church leaders. We all are leaders. We all are leaders at one time or another, even if just in our household. So as a leader, specifically as a leader in the church, my dissertation was geared toward strengthening the covenant relationship. In it, I assert that one way to strengthen the covenant relationship is through green burials, by paying attention to the earth and to the land. So, this was my angle or anchor (if you will) in my dissertation to say that this, the green funeral, is one way of strengthening covenantal relationships. Of course, there's plenty of ways one can strengthen a covenant, through (1) prayer, and

(2) witnessing, for example. But I argued for the green burial. Let us look to and pay attention to the environment, not just the recycling of plastic. But as I stated to give life and being more life giving in death and inside of funerals.

Wilson: You make it sound so easy! It's like, why don't others just get it? Please know that your literature is a testament to how to balance the relationship between God, the creator and the environment and why it's so necessary. This story just popped into my head. I was very close with my grandmother, Mama Ruby. She transitioned three years ago in August. Her transition happened rather quickly. We didn't see it coming and she was able to die at home around family, which is a blessing. So, my mother was tasked with the arrangements and I, as her eldest child, was tasked to help her carry out a lot of what Mama Ruby wanted. My mother asked me because she knew how big I was on natural burial. My mother asked me, "What do you want to do? Do you want to go ahead with a natural burial?" I said, "Well let's look into green burial options in Nashville, Tennessee." We found a lady and although she reviewed our local green burial options, I ended up declining it. Now years later, I regret it. Then, I wanted to appease the family with a wake and a viewing. If we had gone with the green burial route, (I understood that) we would not have been able to have an open casket funeral and the funeral would have moved a lot quicker than what my family was ready for. In addition, my mother said, "You know, your grandmother knew a lot of people who loved her."

It meant or translated to me that people would want to see her and spend time with her inside of a traditional (official) viewing of the body. (Which I believed could only be done if the body was embalmed.) So, to appease everybody, I went ahead and said, "Well Mama, let's just go the conventional route." But today, I hate that I did that because I find it to be so much more meaningful to go about it the way that God designed for us to go about it: we're putting that body back in the ground (the re-grounding). But what did bring me a sense of peace is that I was able to cut a little piece of her hair off. Later, when my children and I went to Kilimanjaro in Africa, I placed a little piece of her in that African soil. Africa was somewhere that my grandmother and I always talked about. So currently there is a barrier between the Black Church and Black community with the green funerals that I wish to remove and to make it normalized. But as an engineer, please tell me from an engineer's perspective, and an academic scholar, how might we implement the green funeral more? Maybe it would be in conjunction with science class. But in our academic institutions, is there a way that we could kind of soften the blow of talking death to students, to young people? Well, you know it's all about education. But what grade level do you say should we start introducing topics of death? Being that we feel that this topic is worthy of discussion in our school systems, but at what age?

Dawson: Education is always the key. Start training and education at the house with mothers and fathers sitting down and not being afraid to talk. Yet knowing *when* is critical. Knowing when your child is mature enough to understand, if not all, pieces. Knowing that one child may grow at a different rate than the next child, it is not a one size fits all. Parents might have to introduce death conversations differently (creatively), in a different way for one child to the next. Like sex education, having death conversations as part of the standard education curriculum within the school system would be excellent. But I can't take the responsibility off the parent. The responsibility will always fall back on or come back to the parents to talk and present this conversation early and in a palatable way with your child, understanding/adapting the mentality that death what is a part of life, right? Death happens and it's gonna happen. Yet, I understand that death is a very tender topic that very young children won't understand. For example: if something happens to mom or dad, often, the child's first reaction is, What do you mean he or she is not coming back, right? The mom or dad just went to work. We go and come every day. We go and we come back. We go and we come back. The child is perplexed. "What do you mean? I don't understand." Again, death conversations are best to have at the house for the parents to decide when is a good time to introduce death, to have the talk.

Wilson: Yes, my children are ten and fifteen. They have been around long enough to see a lot of the deaths in our family and around our family. So, I've found it to be effective for us to have conversations about death. I tell them "Listen, when daddy goes, and I'm not married you are in charge. You know daddy wants to go back into the ground naturally. I want to be a part of the earth." I always tell them, "I want a mango tree over me." Mangos are my favorite. I want my grandkids to eat from their mango tree. [Laughing]. Like this is my granddaddy [Laughing]. So yes, talking to them about it and in that way, it makes them more receptive to the idea of death. Talking to them about natural burial having more than one meaning. We understand the emotional detachment but also speak to the giving back. (Giving back where now the ground, the ecosystem, can feed from us.) So, that's one thing that me and my children do.

But I think that's a very good point that you brought up about having these *tender conversations.* Because you're right, you know, most people don't want to talk about it [death]. Yet, I believe if it's presented the right way; a way that meets you where you are. Early conversations could be very effective in sculpting [young] minds toward normalization. So, I appreciate you bringing that up. I just appreciate your overall work in this area because (like I said) in the sector of burials and bereavement, due to little to no representation. One thing in this country we talk about is representation and having Black representation. Yet, we don't have a lot of Black representation in this important area where I believe we have a lot to say.

Let's go back. You mentioned the land. Land has been [and still is] the focal point of so much in this world. We should get back as a global Black community to recognizing the importance of the land. God is not making no more land. Making use of the fertile soil to grow our crops. That is something else that I often talk about (although I don't mean to ramble) but like you know the nutritiousness (I don't know if I made that word up) but the level of nutrition of our fruits and vegetables depends a lot on what's in the ground; and if we're not replenishing and enriching that soul as we should, our future generations could be faced with a food shortage. You know, already, in the Black communities, food deserts are prevalent.

Dawson: I wish to touch on specific considerations regarding green burials. But please hold me to the land conversation. As a former member of the Green Burial Council, there are conversations that surround a new approach to cemeteries and making them a little differently; making our cemeteries, our burial grounds, our natural burial grounds, with a park feel; [Wilson: "umm"] to not simply consider the burial ground as being *over there* someway in the distance [a place we go to grieve] but to make burial ground more family friendly; maybe with a park feel. Go, have some chairs or let's go to walk the dog. Let's go over there and do things more often. Let's have walking trails. So, I just wanted to share that a redesign of cemeteries (burial grounds) is of consideration and conversation. Now, getting back to the land. Who owns the land? What you see now, are landowners getting on the bandwagon of this green burial. [FACTS] Who owns the most land in America? The white people are the majority in land ownership, true. Now, they are coming and bringing this natural [green] burial concept back to us [Black folk]. They want the Black folks to get to know about this [concept of green burial]. For me this is where it gets a little dicey. Now if one is not careful, they're bringing it to us and saying if you pay us this price, you can be buried here, right? Don't think that the green burial is the least expensive option because for you to be buried in a certain spot being in a green place can cost you. So, if you're not careful there are some [as in many different scenarios] that have the sweetest intentions. I'm not putting anyone down, right. I'm just saying, please have your antennas up, Black folks if you want to get on this bandwagon. It may all very well be good. My unrest is with the continuation of us as Black folks being sold something that in some cases was ours from the beginning. But the powers to be never made amends to what was taken, or the government reneged on our forty acres and a mule. Which very well in some cases now has become these beautiful rolling hills now being showcased in green burials. These thoughts are not toward everybody or one, just a thought of mine. History shows that land was swindled away from Black people; now, the majority owners are coming back around and selling us the ground, right. We see this day after day after day in different sectors of society. Yet again that's not everybody. But I would say to the Green Burial Council (GBC) and the people advocating for green burials to do your research of the land of these burial sites and approach the Black community with care because (for me) this is "the" very delicate topic. Then (in general) I have heard it said that "Black folks always want something given to them." Some own all these rolling hills but where'd you get it from? Some seek a divine place to rest in death and some seek generational wealth. (I don't mean to ramble) but that's why I encourage the GBC and the landowners to do the research of your own land before seeking the buy-in of others. For many, burials and burial grounds are sacred. So let us have divine intentions. So, stay woke Black Church, Black community. Go after/Seek your own land, right. Go and talk, have a conversation with your local city council people, the local land trust people in your own area to find out about who owns the land and the history of property. It may have well been your relative's property. Advocate for your land. Advocate for the "forty acres and a mule" and everything else that is rightfully owned. Advocate, be a part of our moving forward. Stop sitting back. Advocate for us.

Wilson: YES! And to the last point. My father died before I was born. He was buried in a Black cemetery in Nashville, Tennessee, in the traditional manner. I often toyed with the notion of maybe having my dad dug up just, in an effort to make known my sentiments with the environment. Because I have a direct say so in regard to him, I was thinking that maybe I should have him dug up and not take up or occupy that [traditional] space in the ground anymore. But please let me ask you this in relation to the green burial council, are there options out there for those of us who do know and want to make strides to contribute positively in a natural way, are there options of possibly digging up a loved one or doing something to have them removed [from the traditional burial plot]? I don't know if they can't be naturally buried anymore because they have been embalmed. But is it any type of way [possible] that we can remove them and do something else? What do you think?

Dawson: The laws of the state govern what you can do. Your local mortician should be able to assist with this answer. Yet, remember we talked about *per state*. This is not a federal conversation with set laws across the board. So, have conversations with your local morticians, and your state representatives about what you can do now. Please know that there are levels to green burials. I believe you said your grandmother died at home.

Wilson: Yes ma'am

Dawson: So, when we talk about family participation, that is something the Green Bureau Council speaks of a lot and advocates for more family input. Input for a green (natural) burial might include the washing of the body or not; one can help transport the body or not; you can make use of a hearse or not; use a horse; preferably use a casket with natural materials not artificial but biodegradable. It is preferred to use materials such as a wood casket, a woven basket, or a shroud. You, the family, can dig the grave. No professional grave diggers needed. You can go dig on the designated plot on the burial ground and place your loved one there. So, simply know that there exist levels or options of this thing call greening death (and green funeral). Decide what you want to do and what you don't want to do. Know your options, find out, educate yourself per your state and then decide what you want to do.

Wilson: Yes ma'am! I appreciate it very much! Mrs. Dawson.

6

In House Beauty, Everyday Beauty

Called to the Ground—Beauty in Gardening

JESUS IS ALWAYS earnestly and tenderly calling. As a child, I would see my grandmother gardening and if I was inside, I always tried to go outside with her. I would get down in the rows with her and ask her, "What are you doing?" I could clearly see that she was tending to the garden, but I literally got in her way and wanted to know specifics. She would say, "You see what I am doing. I'm digging these potatoes up." or, "I'm pulling these dead leaves off the collards because the bugs have gotten to them." Back then I never had a desire to garden or anything that had to do with putting my hands in the dirt. I thought gardening and placing one's hand in the ground was for old people. I thought that because my grandma was home all the time, that it was a part of her home duties. Certainly, this was one way she showed her love and care for us. As an adult, going through life's ups and down, hills and valleys, I was called to the ground. Again, I never saw myself as one for "yard" anything but as a homeowner there is always work to do inside and outside of the house. Around the outside of the house needed tending—the shrubs were not trimmed evenly, the weeds were out of control, the grass had overgrown its bounds and the landscaping was nonexistent. In other words, the outside of the house, at that time, was representative of what was going on inside of the house. In the midst of chaos and confusion, gardening, the act of putting my hands in the ground, created peace in a way that I never knew existed; and that I never wished to entertain. I never had a desire to garden. I was a computer scientist, so I paid to have someone come and do the work. I worked inside the house, at a desk, and not outside in the dirt. I was relatively young and vibrant. I only played in the dirt. Yet, there in the ground, in the soil, I found the network of minerals and nutrients for the earth, for my soul—soul to soil and soil to soil. Literally, the more I dug down and cut back the hedges (literally and figuratively—decluttering) the more I could see the richness of the soil and there I gained a real appreciation of complex mechanisms and organisms, processes, methodologies, and networking that however taught in school, it was not until I was called to the ground (literally) that the processes of life began to center themselves as meaningful. God said I'm going to use everything that you have been through for my glory. Nothing shall be wasted. All has been uniquely designed for me. There is a prepared seat for those that have been processed and prepared to one day sit with God in glory (Mark 10:40). But before then, here on earth God shall make use of the ups and the downs.

Often, how a yard is kept is critical to the beauty of the entire community. But sometimes the comparison to a neighbor's yard can render one weak, overwhelmed, and can be discouraging, causing one to not begin the process at all. But to begin the process, although the way may seem daunting yet with consistency in effort, one will discover a wholeness, the peace, the shalom, that in some way aids in soothing all things. So, I chose to garden and not compare, garden as if no one is looking.

Called To The Farm: Beauty In a Goat

Only certain kinds of things can be cast out through fasting and praying. (see Mark 9:29)

Throughout my life, I've noticed a fear in several things: being under water (so the thought of baptism was terrifying), the loud shouts of military drill sergeants in military training (unlike the soft yet stern voice from my home training) and the fear of gardening—coming in contact with bugs and other creatures of the soil. I also feared "healthy" eating. I perceived healthy food as tasting bad; the best foods were usually the sweetest. I knew that I could eat, at times, uncontrollably, and I had to get my eating under control. For this challenge, the Lord has granted me favor through fasting and prayer.

While I was in divinity school, I had to face my fear of eating healthy and reconstruct my sense of what I thought of as *good food.* On a retreat for pastors and preachers, I ventured with classmates to Thunder Mountain, discovering newness of life around the table. The retreat, "Life Around the Table: Come to the Table," presented a holistic view of eating and farming. The Life Around the Table platform promoted open-mindedness regarding land, faith, eating, and Sabbath. In this experience, we also met Howard, Howard the goat. Howard has a disorder that causes him to faint when excited or scared. His muscles become tense. Howard falls over, and after approximately ten seconds, he simply goes on his way again. Howard impressed me as I sought to learn from his getting up again. Never mind the fact that Howard is a goat! (BTW—Howard was my biological father's name.) Yet, what could I learn from Howard the fainting goat? As I saw him arise, *do not faint,* I thought, do not fall down in fear. Galatians 6:9 pushes me not to grow weary or faint in well doing. Psalm 27:13 (KJV) says, "I had fainted, unless I had believed to see the goodness of the Lord in the land of the living." This psalm encourages me not to lose heart, not to faint, but to recognize and to embody the goodness of the Lord in everyday things, even in a fainting goat. In this experience, and in our learning about food and faith, I knew that God was setting me free from the chain of chicken. Later, when I went to Buffalo Wild Wings and Popeye's, two of my favorite places, the chicken tasted nasty. Over time my taste for chicken has returned, but since my encounter with Howard on the mountain, I have been able to enjoy this indulgence with moderation.

Fasting and Praying

I sought the Lord, and he heard me, and delivered me from all my fears. (Ps 34:4)

Oh Yes! I cannot just run my body to physical exhaustion! Taking care of the body in the natural, might I compare this care to the spiritual? Do I take care of the Lord's business the way I take care of the business of working out, eating, and earning the "mighty dollar" or human approval? Do I have Christ's approval: child well done? Today as I Keep God First, it is crucial to remember Christ and engage in kingdom-hearted business, as well as properly nourishing my physical body. Amen.

I was afraid to break the chain of sugar, chicken (meat), and other guilty culinary pleasures. I feared that I would not like changing my foods, faith, finances, family, and fitness habits. However, I now see these healthier living practices and intentional lifestyle adjustments have made for a better me. Despite my fears, I chose healthier practices, and I stuck with them for forty days. After forty days, my changes became a new lifestyle. When I set aside a poor choice, I learned that I would see holy things more clearly. Seeking God's face—not God's hand—inside of fasting and praying, has restored my twenty-twenty vision. God shone glory on things and places that earlier I could not see, even something as mundane as how sugar affects the body God gave me, how it made me feel. As I exchanged unhealthy habits for healthy ones, I could see where I could be a light to others and be healthier for the tasks that God has assigned for my hands. I cannot go back to the way I used to be. Fasting isn't a diet; it's about living better for the kingdom. Now, the goal is to carry the fast over into everyday living. My body is a temple, and I will treat it as such.

Beauty in Fasting

Fasting creates space to get in touch (or back in touch) with what really matters; and as quality assurance specialists would say "remove the waste," to declutter so we can best call and recall, to think and rethink, to condition and recondition, to engineer and reengineer to imagine and reimagine our future and our family's future. Fasting can help you shed off the dead excessive weight of the world and to usher you clearly and cleanly into the things of God. Simply put, fasting can cultivate a peaceful mind, (look at the birds) a serene and joyful heart, in the midst of despair, toward a transformative journey of self-discovery, the discovery of new food, a new appreciation of outdoors, and stillness, as never before. All-the-while FASTING is helping you fight battles from a power position. Fasting can change a view or a perspective; when you are looking for one thing, God will do something else. You could look for God to change a person, place, or thing and God can certainly do that BUT God will change you inside of the thing. The gospels of Mark and Matthew are clear when Jesus said that some things can only be done through prayer and fasting. Matthew points to the birds, not as a crazy gaze but as an indication of God's provision. Matthew says to consider the lilies as God's providence; how God's keeping power is true. So, then we too must trust God with our lives. God said, I shall remember the land. We should put our trust in God and sing: "And we trust God as the greatest power and we shall never, never be defeated." No matter what it looks like; the enemy comes to test your faith. "And we trust God the greatest power and we shall never, never be defeated."

Called to Journal: Beauty in Writing Like No One Is Watching

> *Now unto him that is able to do exceedingly abundantly above all that we ask or think, according to the power that worketh in us.* (Eph 3:20 KJV)

A spiritual advisor asked me to journal, to privately take notes of my life and what God was doing. I refused. Years later in divinity school, I was again asked by a professor to journal. Inside myself, I refused. Yet this time, journaling was an in-class assignment and he was walking around checking to see who was doing the work. As with full immersion water baptism, I had to relinquish my anxiety—the anxiety of someone seeing what I was writing; the anxiety of someone knowing my actual thoughts. Yet this was an opportunity for me to be made free. Journaling was a chain that had me bound. But I had to refuse to be bound. I had to want to be free of the chains of others knowing, of someone looking and reading me. In the classroom moment, I decided to be freed. Fearlessly, I channeled my energies toward structured, radical writing. I wrote as if no one was looking. I wrote things in my journal that I never told anyone. I wrote about visiting a farm and how this visit came on the heels of my biological father's death—that part. I wrote about Howard, the fainting goat at a farm, but how I disclosed that in fact Howard was my dad's name and how I found healing on the farm by touching and looking into Howard's eyes before Howard the goat fainted. And of course, Howard the goat would later stand back up again. It was as if Howard was a sign of inner strength; that when one falls, fails, or is fractured, there is a getting back up inside. Profound because in life, I thought of my dad not as the G-O-A-T (greatest of all time) but as a billy goat, stubborn, not taking ownership and responsibility, having every reason in the world to be absent as a dad. I had no clue of how much that outside adventure was going to be therapeutic, but it was.

In class, as I wrote, I observed that my chain of suffering over my absentee father was continually being lifted in the most unlikely places, even in the metaphor of a fainting goat.

God has a way of healing, delivering and setting free that I nor anyone could have possibly imagined. All I had to do was to be in place and do what I was being asked to do. Freedom! The Spirit revealed that serving God means being free from fear, seeking a better love of Christ, and now, following my desire to write.

Called to Veterans: The Beauty in Story

Part of that desire to write is the recognition that written stories have power. As a veteran, I know that veterans like to have their stories told. I love hearing their stories. When I go to a VA hospital, I intentionally listen to veterans and encourage their steadfastness regarding service-connected illnesses and injuries. I encourage family members of disabled veterans to tell, or to help tell, the veteran's story. I have seen relatives, many times over, tell veterans' stories in their presence. The veterans' reactions show that hearing their stories told does those veterans' hearts worlds of good. Seeing elderly veterans at memorial sites receiving honors or medals when their stories have been told or recognized is a sight to behold. Those veterans experience such a sweet spot. Hearing and encouraging family members and others to write down these stories is part of my ministry, just as studying biblical stories and sharing insights is. Writing, for me, is a part of reckoning with my story, to move forward.

Call to Worship: Beautiful Worship Like No One Is Looking

Be not afraid of their faces: for I am with thee to deliver thee, saith the Lord. (Jer 1:8 KJV)

In the face of my fears about writing, holy boldness was my prayer. Not only did I have to face my fear of writing, I also had to relinquish anxieties around those who see me and I know are watching. I had to let go of the distractions. I had to stop wondering what people were going to think, what they might say, whether my praise would be socially acceptable, or if my acclamations of Amen were too loud. My list could go on and on. I felt like Peter being freed from prison in Acts 12. I could be free to praise the Lord, free from captivity to people's opinions, and free from the prison guards that have a hold on my praise.

Oh yes! There is a time of praise! I praise in part because of my release from fear. God not only said, "I will go down with you," but, "I will also surely bring you up again" (Gen 46:4). God is definite in forward thinking. God moves toward renewal and restoration, as I saw in confronting each of my fears. God sent Israel and his children to Egypt. Perhaps they feared that they would never see their lands again. But God sent word through Joseph: "Then Joseph said to his brothers: I am about to die; but God will surely come to you and bring you up out of this land to the land that he swore to Abraham, to Isaac, and to Jacob," (Gen 50:24–25). Generations later, God declared to Moses, "I have come down to deliver them [Israel] from the Egyptians and to bring them up out of the land to a good and broad land" (Exod 3:8). God then describes, in Micah 2:12 (KJV), "I will surely assemble, O Jacob, all of thee; I will surely gather the remnant of Israel." Again, and again, this same promise echoes through generations. God insisting that God's people be confident in God's very nature as a protector and a promise keeper. God replaced their fears with belief in what God had already spoken and shown through great deeds. Thus, the people praised God! Just as I praise God for empowering me to confidently overcome my fears, I ask others: what holds you back? What fears keep us stuck, afraid to move forward?

God Is Continually Calling and Grounding

> *Greater is He that is within me, than he that is in the world.* (see 1 John 4:4)

I never knew the depths of God's love until I faced my fears. I have learned that my oceans are never so deep that God is not with me. Since God's kingdom has not fully come on earth, in my ministry, or within me, I still have work to do and have room for growth. I know that I am growing in grace and seek to practice overcoming fear and turning to praise. For practices are signs of kingdom mindedness and an openness for God to work God in you. In church, I come to worship God. I do not want to spend my call to worship on anxiety about what other people see, think, or say. My call requires me to embody what I have been preaching. Embodiment may be a recent theological concept, but the idea is the same from days of old, "You got to live holy." By practicing, that is, the Christian's practice, I mean holiness, acting in the way of the Lord. Acting as Jesus would act and doing what Jesus would do.

As I move forward, I look back and see how God was setting me up for Christ's glory. For you who know that God has a purpose for your life—let my story sink into the imagination, take root and grow. To clear your mental ground for spiritual growth, you may have to face your fears. I urge readers to probe deeper into the things of Christ and to let this appeal resonate. Where do we need to surrender thoughts, money, and energies to God?

Let us fix our minds on the things above and not waste our call to worship. We need only to live out the Gospel, knowing that our God is simply able. By God's ability, we move forward.

God will never stop calling us toward greater; toward Godself, even in death. May we be more beautiful than ever before willingly engage in and with creation in strengthening our resolve for the things of God without fear.

Beauty in Visitation: Who Did the Body?

Preservation and Beauty

"The grass withers and the flower fades," the Bible proclaims in Isaiah 40:7 and 1 Peter 1:24. Yet, as we age or when death arrives, people (our bonds, emotions, and feelings) need a minute, sometimes days, or at times, years, to catch up with what God is doing (or has allowed). Aesthetics—what one values, appreciates, and finds beautiful—are relative at least, and intimate and personal, at most. Being able to look beyond what one can see—by tapping into the spirit and the spiritual—is needed more often than seeing with our physical sight. But does physical sight help or hinder us from getting to the space of acceptance and peace? Often, beauty (by way of colonialism and capitalism) has misplaced the concept of beauty toward the tangible and the corruptible. However, I find beauty in visiting the sick. My care for those with a spirit of infirmity does not stop when the last breath was taken. I still care. As a minister to bereaved families, I've become observant of the dead and the processes of funeralization that operate as a continuation of the relationship that has been built during visitations. Ultimately, my staying close with them (for me) meant staying close to God whom I now believe is the keeper of those that have died in the Lord. I want to get closer to what God, and to where God, wants us to be in relation to funerals. This closeness lies in keeping our eyes on God even as we look upon, not only the dead, but also what we consider as beauty in life. And death is a part of life.

Embalming, (the preservation of the deceased,) allows time for people to process death. My concern with embalming, as we know it, is with the larger ecological implications of the picture being painted and any harm that is being done to the earth—the people and the environment. At the start of my ministry, I wrote "The Beauty in Visitation" because I never wanted to forget what visitation and the people meant to me. At that time, I was not educated on environmentalism, toxicity in death practices, or earth theology; so, my thoughts then were not where I'd wish them to be now, but nonetheless my thoughts were my thoughts and maybe an indication of the thoughts of others, and of God working in me toward a clearer vision (a new lens) in which to view death practices. Here, I share that student essay with you in hopes of adjusting or raising awareness as one considers what is beautiful.

The Beauty in Visitation

"I'm so ugly!" Ms. Ruby proclaimed as she reflected on her aged face, which now displayed a smile and a few missing teeth. Such a precious jewel, Ms. Ruby, diagnosed with heart disease, failing eyesight, and currently bedridden, pointed to a picture of herself on the wall in her assigned room at the nursing home. In that picture, she had to be in her late twenties or early thirties, standing tall in a pretty skirt with a hand placed intentionally on her hip. In that picture, she appeared to be going up the stairs of the porch to her home. She appeared to be entering her home, a place where love abounds and where people are gathered and await your return, your entrance. In that picture, there was no sign of pain or suffering. Death was nowhere to be found, just howdy-howdy. There she declared her beauty as if she longed for those days once more. Who would not want to go back home?

Oh Yes! I thought. "The picture is lovely." However, as I looked at her, I did not see the *ugly* lying before me. As a minister there to serve inside of visitation, my mind, heart, and eyes were fixed on seeing Jesus. But as a human being, could I somehow understand her words? Could I possibly relate to her feelings? My Grandma Duke used to say, "beauty fades and ugly [yes, ugly] holds its own." At that time, I had no idea that some of grandma's words held biblical connotations. Interesting how life inevitably ushers us into what is important, what is really beautiful, like a picture of home. The symbol of home truly functions.

The Beauty of Holiness The old preacher teaches that ministry is serious business where the lives of people are at stake. When, in critical times, people want to see Jesus. In critical times, one believes that the servant of God (in whom we call) has been in communion with the Lord and can speak to God on one's behalf through intercessory prayer. Critical times in a hospital or nursing home when one is away from family and away from things that are familiar, there is space for huge adjustment. These spaces yield heightened senses and desires for God to intervene on one's behalf. Ministry calls for its representatives to seek God like never before—even before serving, before the laying-on of hands (touching someone and praying over them), before the visitation. There is something beautiful about centering oneself in prayer and praise, in dialogue with God, calling on the name of Jesus, listening then following God's instruction; then stepping out.

For the minister, it is imperative that one prepares and is intentional about living holy in efforts that God will honor the human effort and will do the supernatural with our efforts. With prayer and fasting—a most powerful spiritual discipline, I engage in ministry. These acts translate into a lifestyle of fasting and praying, seeking God's face—for his glory, for direction and not his hand, making God into a personal *gofer*. In prayer, God is to be exalted and thanked for his goodness. I ask for forgiveness of my sins and for deeper discernment. It is something simply beautiful about living a holy life. With God's help, one is ready to visit, to minister to others and to intercede on the behalf of others. From there, one can step out into ministry in the beauty of holiness asking God to allow the envisioning even further of what the natural eye can see. It is there inside of visitation; I wish desperately for the people to hear from heaven; and most of all, to receive Christ in one's heart and to be drawn closer to God as never before. Through the reading of a daily devotion, scripture, prayer, friendly conversation, a touch or a song, Christ is lifted to ease all the heavy burdens.

During this season with Ms. Ruby, I participated in visitation weekly. Even in my brokenness, I found strength as I reached toward heaven on their behalf as I prepared for the week, for the day. I would pray calling out a name one by one unto the Lord asking God to do the impossible, the miraculous, the things I cannot do, all before I get to the physical place of visitation, my God-given assignment. As I go on the visitations, I go to meet Jesus; to see God in all things. So, as I entered, I saw the tangible things and the people, yet I didn't. I was looking intentionally to see Jesus, looking further than what my eyes could see.

Before entering the building, I speak to God a final time. With my prayer partner(s), we would touch and agree and pray "in the name of Jesus let the people see you." That is the place and space I was in when Ms. Ruby shared her deep thoughts about herself.

The Beauty in Relationship I got to know Ms. Ruby and the others assigned during this season of visitation. In that season, hospital visits were made as needed but those that were *sick and shut-in*—as called in the olden days—were routinely scheduled and visited. I would wake up knowing who would probably be on the list to see that day: Ms. Ruby, Ms. Hazel, and/or Mr. David. I would get excited to see each person. They too would be waiting and expecting the visit. I remember the uniqueness of each person. Many things stood out for various reasons. I developed real relationships with these people.

Ms. Ruby moved from one nursing home to another. At one place she complained about the workers and the food. She became so flustered that with the help of her family members, she moved to a new nursing home facility. She appeared to like this new place a lot better. It appears these nursing homes or assisted living facilities are trial-and-error. One must find the right place for them and their situation. But before she moved, Ms. Ruby was in the nursing home with Ms. Hazel listed on the regularly scheduled visitation list. They knew we were coming. Together yet individually, each would wait for their specialized visit.

Ms. Hazel was wheelchair bound and ate little to nothing. She was bone thin yet could muster up enough strength to roll herself around in the wheelchair and then point, reflecting on a picture of herself with her sisters on the wall of her assigned room. Pictures on display are great points of engagement during every visitation. I watch as the person comes to life inside of the picture.

Mr. David would always sit quietly awaiting a visit from his wife of over sixty years. He knew that every day she would come. "I'm waiting on Margret," he would say. "She is on her way." Every time, if Margret was not already there, he would be waiting for her to return. For Mr. David, his wife, her cooking, and their children would be our talking points of interest. He loved to talk about anything that included Margret.

Ms. Ruby loved to eat. She loved fruit and would ask us to bring it. One year, before she became totally bedridden, in addition to fruit, she asked for a coat. Not ever wanting to disappoint, we knew never to make promises to bring anything. But my heart wanted so much to get her that coat. But everyone's situation is so uniquely different. However, there was one promise made at the end of each visit, the promise to come back: "We'll be back to see you." Due to a shift in church assignments, I did not visit Ms. Ruby nor the others from that season as often as before. However, I understood they asked about me and I would ask about them because in those scenes of our lives, somehow, we build eternity, we build relationships with each other but also with the Lord.

The Beauty of Knowing the Lord

Being associated with the same church, most all the people we visited knew the Lord. Knowing the Lord makes the visit very pleasant. However, we would find people at different places in their walk with the Lord. But at that season in life, each of those visited all needed encouragement and at times, reassuring. Often, during the visitation whether in the hospital, nursing home, or at a residence, the scriptures would be read, and friendly conversation would be shared. From one bedside to the next, we would travel. For me, one of the highlights was communion. The sharing of Christ's body and blood and remembering the Lord until he comes. Often before leaving, we would sing the songs of Zion. It would only be three or four of us singing but such precious memories were made.

We knew the presence of the Lord made the difference and the supernatural possible, even if every note was not perfect. When a person knows and confesses Jesus Christ as Lord, we have something to be happy about and to celebrate. We are saved from the penalty of sin. Death and the grave have no victory in the life of a Christian. The last time I saw Ms. Ruby in October, not only did she point (again) to the picture, but she also shared a feeling about of not making it to the New Year. We assured her of God's promise to never leave nor forsake her. We took communion and sang the songs of Zion. Ms. Ruby knew the Lord, so therefore, we rejoiced.

Ms. Ruby did make it to see the New Year and the New Year after. But just into that New Year, in January, I received the word that Ms. Ruby had passed, gone home to be with the Lord. The word came of Ms. Ruby's departure just like it had for the others: Ms. Hazel, Mr. David, and now Ms. Ruby.

The Beauty in Death: Gone Home

After her passing, I was told that Ms. Ruby was ready to go home to be with the Lord. Upon hearing of her passing, I went to Ms. Ruby's viewing at the funeral home, a final visitation on this side of glory. As I walked up, on the outside of the door of the funeral home, was a stand that displayed her name. "Yes, that is her," I thought to myself. As I entered the funeral home chapel, I noticed the open casket then I was immediately greeted by a representative. I signed the guest book, as I did every time I visited her in the nursing home. From the back of the small chapel, I began to walk toward the casket. From the building and from the casket, lights shone down on her. From the back of this chapel, I began to see a beautiful woman lying in peace. I began to walk toward her, toward that beautiful peace. I finally reached her casket side. She was dressed in winter white with her hair pulled back. She was adorned in pearl earrings.

I imagine the heavenly home with the Lord where there is always howdy-howdy and never goodbye, and "there are pleasures forever more" (Ps 16:11 KJV). There is where Ms. Ruby longed to be, a place very close to God. Now, there she is in the presence of the Lord where there was fullness of joy (Ps 16:11) and eternal life, with no more pain and sorrow. Who wouldn't want to go home? This belief, this trust in the Lord made this final visitation for Ms. Ruby one of beauty. I knew I must look beyond what my eyes could see. In my humanness, I will miss her. My heart is saddened, and I cried but there is hope. At this time and in this moment, I must look beyond my own failing eyes, my broken heart and beyond the hills to see Jesus. Jesus makes it all beautiful. I trust that Ms. Ruby is now home with the Lord.

Yes, Ms. Ruby, and the others of that season, have all gone home. I did not attend the actual homegoing services of either of the three but notably, Mr. David's wife passed before he did. Then, I attended the funeral for Mr. David's wife where Mr. David was in attendance. The church is full of people paying their final respects. The service was nicely done with singing and with words of comfort. Notably, this service was one of the rare occurrences where the body of the deceased was fully displayed, where the casket top was completely opened. Mr. David's wife was dressed to the nines (meaning she was *sharp*—adorned in a beautiful dress and stockings). On her feet, she had on pumps as if she could, at any moment, get up and step out. I understand that the funeral home requests the body to be fully clothed down to the undergarments. No doubt, the funeral home attempts to make the final viewing one that reminds the family of life. Yet, in real time (in the moment) to what extent does this preservation alter or take away from the wellness and wholesomeness of creation? Assumingly, the funeral home employees have already been exposed to toxics through the embalming process, the funeral service attendees are now exposed to and experiencing a glorified body that is dressed to the nines (casket sharp), and the ground awaits the tons of man-made materials to be place in it. All these hinder the natural decomposition process.

Now, not only do I look back as I write in humble submission to the Almighty God—the One who knows all and who sees all, the One who can eternally perfect the work of visitation—but I thank God for allowing me to enter the private spaces, the precious scenes in the lives of God's people; and in such a vital way, knowing that those precious people impacted my life, as well, in a very real way. Ugly, Oh No! God makes all things new.

But, now that we have the green funeral, which seeks to aid in the strengthening of my covenant relationship with God, it behooves us to keep God in our hearts and minds above what we see. Ultimately, trusting in the Creator to reconcile all things unto Godself, yet all the while, ensuring that we do our part—from the time of death to disposition—to not allow or play into capitalism or our own vain glory of beauty and the swaying of our attention away from the grass withering and the flower fading, even at the apex of our emotions. We can do a better job.

Let us insist on options, having access to options, that remove toxins from our funeral processing. Let us educate ourselves and others on what it takes to be better stewards of the earth and creation. Let us work internally on ourselves to help move us away from our capitalistic ways of thinking and of being toward a new life and life more abundantly, even in death and funeral processing.

7

Staying Woke in Death

At the End of the Day

AS STATED PREVIOUSLY, as a minister of the gospel, a director of bereavement, and a chaplain within the health care system, I have been called to the bedside of those who are reported to be actively dying. Actively dying signifies the final stage of dying when the patient is expected to die within a matter of hours or days, usually within three days. This could be considered an application of "at the end of a day"—when the moral or temporal body is at the end of life. At the end of the day, what matters to the Black Church? Dean David Goatley asserts that "what we do, implicitly or explicitly, affects all around us; to include the care or corruption of creation." Like John in Revelation, Goatley asserts, there is more to see than what is seen with the ordinary or natural eye. Davis in *Scripture, Culture, and Agriculture* suggests that there is a way of seeing that is bifocal—having the near sight on what is imminent then a long-term vision of the day of the Lord, the day of reckoning. Goatley would suggest in preparation for the end of the day it is advantageous for the Black Church to "seek discipline and discernment to faithfully follow the will of God as we await the return of Christ Jesus." The embodiment of an ecological theology through creation care is what a proactive wait resembles, what Dean Gregory Jones would consider as "pushing-off from our tiptoes and not reacting from our heels." The green funeral is an alternative to the toxic traditional funeral practices that invites the Black Church to push-off from our tiptoes and not react from our heels because the end of the day is nearing.

This book aims to raise the consciousness of Black churches around environmental theology that will result in discouraging toxic burial practices and embracing the environmentally friendly practices of green funerals by answering three fundamental questions:

1. How might better attention to environmentalism help Black churches, ecclesial leaders and families to understand better the toxic impact of traditional funeral practices on creation?
2. How might better attention to environmental theology help Black churches, ecclesial leaders and families to seek alternatives to environmental degradation from traditional funeral practices?
3. How might better attention to environmentalism cause churches to reconsider all their material practices so that they might seek to embody holiness and promote beauty relative to creation in all that they do?

A Call to Stay Woke

Suzanne Kelly in *Greening Death* acknowledges "that people are waking up to a deeper yearning—a hunger for more meaningful death practices." I extend this invitation to the Black Church inside of its funeral practices. Theologian James Cone, author of *God of the Oppressed* states "theology should not put us to sleep, but should wake us up!" So, WAKE UP! Do not die, get to higher ground! "Every round goes higher and higher!" RISE, for it is critical that you keep moving forward by seeing yourself in a forward-moving state. People are depending on you! As leaders, it is necessary for the Black Church to find its collective voice on the topics of local and global issues while holding together the tension without damaging its own.

Is this a tall task? Perhaps, but how might the Black Church do this? However painful, the Black Church is obligated to "always be opened and oriented toward freedom," as Herbert R. Marbury in *Pillars of Cloud and Fire* tells us. Expounding on Exodus 13:21–22 ("The Lord went in front of them in a pillar of cloud by day, to lead them along the way, and in a pillar of fire by night, to give them light, so that they might travel by day and by night. Neither the pillar of cloud by day nor the pillar of fire by night left its place in front of the people."), Marbury gives space for the cloud symbol to be subtle and quiet in movement, where appropriate and legitimated by civil society and not as a hiding space to invoke more hurt and pain. In contrast, Marbury interprets the fire as "the symbol invoking a radical challenge to the social and political fabrics of our time."

Although the respective beacons of cloud and fire appeared in vastly different forms, they both led the Children of Israel in the same direction, from slavery toward the Promised Land, and were necessary components of a liberation project. It is not optional for the Black Church to lack in its efforts to exhibit ecological faith. Since its conception, the Black Church has challenged the social and political order of its time. Today, in like fashion, the community needs leaders to include clergy, to lead being the "pillar of cloud by day and a pillar of fire by night." At the end of the day, there is a call for the Black Church to stay woke and to lead—through pandemics, viruses, flus, militarism, racism, sexism, genderism—toward life in the most life-giving ways, even in death.

Green funerals are essential to the practices of Black churches as we continue to meet contemporary challenges. However, green funerals should not be in isolation to other aspects of ministry that help families prepare for the dying aspect of living and honoring God in these critical phases. Green funerals need to fit within a continuum of conversations critical for the Black Church to engage. For example, there is an African American Advanced Planning network that is coordinated by Dr. Patrick Smith and Maria Mugweru. (See Advance Care Planning and Healthy

Living Through Faith at https://tmc.divinity.duke.edu/advance-care-planning-and-healthy-living-through-faith/.)

Additionally, technology raises new questions about artificially extending "life" through technology and the right to die with dignity. (See Activism and End of Life Choice (April)—The Kenan Institute for Ethics at Duke University at https://kenan.ethics.duke.edu/activism-and-end-of-life-choice/.)

With a renewed commitment to environmental theology, the Black Church will be posed to meet and exceed the challenges that are presented in this dissertation.

8

Beauty and Honoring Covenantal Relationships

An Enthroned Mandate: The Glory, Splendor, and Beauty of Creation Care

AS STATED PREVIOUSLY, we must embody an ecology where priesthood means that we lead in the things of God and are co-creatures with other creatures. Community leaders and ecclesial leaders must direct us toward the care of creation and being better stewards of the land. In addition to understanding our connectivity to the land as holy and covenantal, another approach is to guide the Church into its place as a royal priesthood—its beauty, majesty, and splendor (1 Pet 2; Isa 62:3; Deut 7:6). "But ye are a chosen generation, a royal priesthood, a holy nation, a peculiar people; that ye should shew forth the praises of him who hath called you out of darkness into his marvelous light" (1 Pet 2:9 KJV). For the ecclesial leader, what does this look like? As Willie Jennings has stated, we must first recognize that we are *possessed by* and belong to God and so we have limited *possession of* what we claim as our own (see chapter 3). Colossians 1:12–14 says, "giving thanks to the Father, who has enabled [called] you to share in the inheritance of the saints in the light. He has rescued us from the power of darkness and transferred us into the kingdom of his beloved Son, in whom we have redemption, the forgiveness of sins." We are enthroned—sharing in the inheritance—by God's divine power. This enthronement invokes the show of divine love to others—especially the marginalized—the least, the lonely, and the left out. What does it mean to be royal (kingly), enthroned and of royal priesthood? I would argue that that royalty is where the glory of the Lord has been revealed and embodied. For ecclesial leaders, the care of creation rises to this magnitude. God is in communion and fellowship with all forms of the earth. We are in the midst of God's majesty and splendor: the grass of the fields and the flowers of the trees. We must be attentive to the state of the wind, the sea, and the rocks; and what they teach us. The majesty and splendor of God is continual and never ceasing or failing. For many, it does not appear or look like what we would consider as great or of value and may be easily misunderstood. There, we are to spend critical time helping us to fully understand Psalm 24:1 (KJV)—"the earth is the Lord's and the fullness thereof." Let the glory of the Lord rise among us. Let us be transformed and engaged in the metamorphic beauty of God.

As the ecclesial leader engages in the threefold ministry of Christ—prophet, priest, king (sage)—the inclusivity of the community is as royal and vital in the care of creation and as we return to the earth. This displays wisdom. Striving to take care of the ecological health of the world is being kingdom-minded; we are called to use our gifts, care for creation, live side by side with every living thing, and recognize that we, as created beings, are the images of God as holy.

It is royal to be enthroned in what God is, in relationship with and with what God loves. Beauty and splendor cannot be separated from royalty. No matter how it appears to the naked eye. Likewise, God's royalty will never be without glory. Glory is a state that can be bestowed or that can be at rest (when destiny and scripture has been fulfilled) upon such as honor (enthronement). The Messiah was not regal to the natural eye, yet majesty and honor was bestowed from on high: "This is my beloved Son, in whom I am well pleased" (Matt 3:17 KJV). Jesus moved about in sacred quietness or a sanctuary of silence, so when Jesus spoke and acted it drew a multitude. With intentionality, glory can be entered into with praise or a prayer of thanksgiving. A person can raise or be exalted to glory or fall from glory or grace. It is only with a supernatural lifting that the lifting is permanent. There is an element of holiness that rests in glory. One Peter 1:24–25 tells us: "For all flesh is like grass and all its glory like the flower of grass. The grass withers, and the flower falls, but the word of the Lord endures forever." What God deems as beauty is beauty, and what royal is royal.

An Extension of a Marriage: The Black Church and Ecological Faith

It is no coincidence that Jesus's first miracle was performed at a wedding—which creates space for the beautiful bride, the beaded dress, and where love prevails (John 2:1–11). The Black Church is obligated to stop the folly and fumbling with love and to fall in love with creation.

Let us extend the beauty metaphor with covenantal relationship and marry the splendor of the Black Church and ecological faith. Black theological scholars would argue that black folk have never lost their connection to earth and land. I argue that the perceived beauty and goodness of the earth must be remembered, restored, and reclaimed. Just as Ambrose of Milan invites the Church to participate in true beauty, Dr. Betty Holley, associate professor of ecological theology at Payne Theological Seminary, extends an invitation to the Black Church to "an ecological spirituality, to pursue an *ecological conversion*—a transformation that embodies and keeps creation priority on the frontal lobe, and to ultimately protect our home, earth." Holley urges the Black Church to consider their ways and the impact of daily activities on the environment. Most of all, she desires us to know that we all are God's creatures and are indeed tied together. "As a bride adorned for her husband" (Rev 21:2), a wedding analogy can help us in our recommitment to covenant.

Among the rituals of the Church, there is nothing more precious or beautiful than a wedding. As a bride prepares for her husband, "the church is in search of what is beautiful to fit that occasion," says Makoto Fujimura in *Culture Care: Reconnecting with Beauty for Our Common Life*. In preparation for the coming of Christ, for the wedding of God and his church, Fujimura says that God cares about excellence and our attempts to be excellent and faithful will count. The church, like artists and wedding planners, should seek to be best at preparing for this cosmic wedding.

What does beauty have to do with covenantal relationships? Beauty has everything to do with holiness. In Christ, our faith speaks to the mundane and the ordinary. Beauty is to remember what has been lying dormant in your life—areas that need to be awakened that have fallen asleep, that need to be reclaimed. This may require sacrifice, remembering our first love, and taking notes of the current situation—stop seeing pollution and calling it good. It can be argued that if your love is not precious then can it (whatever you have) be called or considered love? Precious love is described in 1 Corinthians 13:4–12, which tells us that, "Love is patient; love is kind; love is not envious or boastful or arrogant or rude. It does not insist on its own way; it is not irritable or resentful; it does not rejoice in wrongdoing but rejoices in the truth. It bears all things, believes all things, hopes all things, endures all things. Love never ends." As a wife is prepared and veiled for her husband, she stands at the altar waiting to be presented—preserved for this moment.

Preservation and Conservation: Covenantal Relationship Extended

Traditionally, the bride is presented in all white as a representation of purity, holiness—nothing lacking, and nothing wasted. How might we prepare humanity as the bride of Christ, holy and acceptable which is our reasonable service? How can we extend holiness inside of a dying process; that we are not toxic, that we are not shown to be lacking in covenant relationship or bordering unbelief? At death, we must stop the separation and injecting of barriers between ourselves and the ground but create a closeness that is beyond the natural eye. Currently, (toxic) preservation starts well before we get to the ground. Embalming and restorative art, which delay the appearance of death, are key factors as the family prepares to view their loved one for the last time. Therein indeed raises challenges for the Black church, its funeral industry, and its community. But the holy preservation and conservation of the earth through creation care is of importance. Dianne Glave and Mark Stoll in *To Love the Wind and the Rain* analyzes how best for the Black Church to honor divine mystery. They argue that one approach is to keep the integration of cultural and nature at the forefront of one's imagination. If you fixate on God's Word and God's promises, then God will fix your feelings about the temporal and carry you toward that which is spiritual and eternal.

With the help of Russian theologian Sergi Bulgakov, Brian Horne in "Divine and Human Creativity" speaks to the character of holiness and art as

> *the revelation of the beautiful already there but undiscovered to the world around us—the true nature of reality, a nature which is usually obscured, hidden, or distorted. But things are transfigured and made luminous by beauty; they become the revelation of their own abstract meaning. And this revelation through beauty of the things of the earth is the work of art.*

Makoto Fujimura describes slow art (when a dry painting brings forth a different texture than when the paint was wet), saying, "Oh how beautiful. The paint had dried and instantly there was a maturity in faith where before there was none." Artists are gifted receptors of the world's woes. For example, the only thing Jesus wore to the cross was Mary's anointing. The centurion would have smelled the aroma—not only the aroma of death but so much more. The centurion, finally concluding, "Truly this man was God's son" (Matt 27:54; Mark 15:39; Luke 23:47).

AFTERWORD

DURING THE SPRING of 2019, I had a feeling something was about to change. I would be entering the writing stage of my doctoral program at Duke University and some version of change was predictable. There was some *other* change, however, that I couldn't predict, but certainly felt. Indeed, I received a phone call that brought about significant change.

Bishop James L. Davis, then-presiding prelate of the Second Episcopal District of the African Methodist Episcopal (AME) Church (a geography that includes Washington, DC, Virginia, and North Carolina) called to offer me an opportunity. He thought I would serve well as the senior pastor of the historic St. Joseph AME Church, in Durham, North Carolina, a congregation established in 1869 and physically located only a few miles from Duke. Although I knew the work would be challenging, I was also extremely excited. Clearly, some things were about to change.

In terms of demographics, I understood from popular rumor that St. Joseph was an "older" congregation. I never thought, however, to *qualify* or *quantify* exactly what "older" meant. Eventually, before Bishop Davis signed my Certificate of Pastoral Appointment, on May 4, 2019, we had a long talk. He shared with me that the Second Episcopal District had done a demographic survey, and he learned St. Joseph's median age was 80. I *understood* what he said, but didn't *comprehend* what he said. As a college student, I studied economics at Howard University. Statistically, therefore, I understood that given the large size of St. Joseph's membership, Bishop Davis was sharing that he was sending me to a very old congregation. What I didn't comprehend, however, was that serving a congregation of such seasoned saints would bring major *changes* to my ministry and role as a minister.

As I began making house visits and meeting with congregants, I met some church members who were in their late eighties. I met others who were in their nineties. During one Sunday morning worship experience, someone even slipped me a note to announce that "Sister Such and Such" would be turning one hundred years old. The congregation erupted in applause. With a nod toward the *munus triplex* doctrine, or the threefold office (exploring Jesus's leadership as a prophet, priest, and king/royal), as much as I naturally gravitated to *prophetic* ministry, given St. Joseph's demographics, I had to grow to become a *priestly* minister, too. In other words, in addition to "speaking truth to power," like a prophet, to successfully serve my congregation, I had to *change*, and grow, to become a priest. When March 2020 came, it presented unforeseen opportunities to grow, as my ministry changed, as I was forced to become a priest.

The COVID-19 pandemic stretched me in unimaginable ways. It apparently also stretched St. Joseph's membership. In twenty-four months, I buried thirty-nine people. Although none of the deaths were COVID-related, I often say, "Father Time is undefeated." Perhaps it was stress. Perhaps it was isolation. Regardless of the cause, I had no choice but to become an expert, of sorts, in the liturgical and homiletical aspects of funerals in the Black Church tradition. After reading *The Green Funeral*, however, I realize I was inept with respect to the *ecological* aspects of funerals. A question, therefore, arises as to whether I am willing to change.

Before I was assigned to St. Joseph, by Bishop Davis, I served under Bishop Julius H. McAllister, Sr., a mentor and friend who often shared, "A celebration of life is for *the living*, more so than for the dead." In *The Green Funeral*, Dr. Sequola Dawson emphasizes the importance of how, in the Black Church's culture, we honor the dead with elaborate funerals. At the same time, however, *The Green Funeral* provides *the living* with opportunities and information, to protect the environment and honor the dead in ecologically meaningful ways. This time, after reading this groundbreaking book, the question arises in the collective context: Are *we* willing to change?

In writing from both conventual and aesthetic perspectives, Dr. Dawson effectively leans into scripture (e.g., Gen 2:7 and Lev 26:42–46), while placing environmental theologians in conversation with one another. By doing so, she has written a groundbreaking work that invites the Black Church into a necessary dialogue about change. *The Green Funeral* makes both the pulpit and pew aware of our ecological crisis and invites the Black Church to change certain things about burial practices that adversely impact the planet. If I had known *then* what I know *now*, not only would the thirty-nine funerals I referenced have been different, but the scores and scores of other funerals I have officiated over my years of pastoral service would have been different, too. I therefore accept *The Green Funeral*'s invitation to honor the dead while also changing the way we bury them.

In meeting with bereaved families, time and time again, I have always seen my role as a *facilitator*, not a director. The role of a pastoral servant is not to *direct* the family in preparing for the funeral. It is to facilitate a space of holy thanksgiving, where the family can make appropriate choices about what's best for them in celebrating their loved one's life. In a similar vein, before I accepted God's call to pastoral service, I was a very successful practicing attorney. Not once did I ever tell a client what to do. Instead, I gave clients options and advised them of likely outcomes, based on the choices before them. *The Green Funeral* equips both clergy members and funeral industry professionals with information that should be used to create choices for families in how they can honor their deceased, while also honoring the land God has entrusted to us (Lev 26:42).

I previously indicated my natural inclination in ministry is prophetic, more so than priestly. Indeed, as a pastor, I have been on the front lines in fighting for voting rights and advocating for various forms of social justice at many public forums. *The Green Funeral* shows that, just as the prophet's role is to challenge existing systems and accepted norms, in planning for a "green funeral," priestly gifted clergy members are also called on to act as prophets, presenting options that can create meaningful change for the betterment of families and the sustainability of Planet Earth.

Bishop Davis's phone call led to unforeseen changes to my ministry. Because I accepted, rather than ran from change, I grew as a pastoral leader. Likewise, reading *The Green Funeral* has also brought change to my ministry. It's changed my perspective, because it's broadened my understanding. If clergy leaders and funeral industry professionals are willing to change, and present ecologically friendly options to families, we can all collectively honor lives that were well-lived and simultaneously protect the environment. To say the least, reading *The Green Funeral* was a "game changer!" I highly recommend it!

Dr. Jonathan C. Augustine
Senior Pastor, St. Joseph AME Church
Durham, North Carolina
February 2025

ACKNOWLEDGMENTS

With all of my love to my daughter Destiny McNeill.

In loving memory of my mother Ethell McNeill and grandmother Leoner McNeill.

Thank you to my pastor, the Reverend Dr. Jonathan C. Augustine; and thank you to my Duke Divinity School First Reader, the Reverend Dr. Emmanuel Goatley.

North Carolina Area Funeral Homes

Honorable Mention

Fayetteville, North Carolina
Wiseman Funeral Home
Tryphina Wiseman
Mrs. Lenora Wiseman
Colvin Funeral Home
Paye Memorial Funeral

Greensboro, North Carolina
Perry Brown Funeral Home
Hargett Funeral Home

Durham, North Carolina
Scarborough Funeral Home
Queen Scarborough
Skippy Scarborough

Dunn, North Carolina
Dafford Funeral Home

Historical Fayetteville, North Carolina
Paye Funeral Home
James "Jimmy" and MayBob Paye
Stephen Rogers Funeral Home
Gilcrest Funeral Home

APPENDIX

SINCE THE CARE of creation is the responsibility of all Christians, the Black Church should desire to take its responsibilities seriously. The Black Church would benefit greatly from further research around religion and ecology, and the work, practices, and commitments of its leaders. The rituals of the Black Church related to death—funerals, memorials, and burial practices funerals—offer opportunities for such fulfillment. I offer a few lingering questions for consideration and continued research:

1. How does the Black Church best work with land trusts and owners to secure property for green burials inside and outside of the Black community?
2. To what extent does ecological sensibilities in African traditional religious thought inform Black Christian thought?
3. Did enslaved people's farming practices and the anticipation of "forty acres and a mule" have theological as well as economic implications?
4. How might emotional attachment to "home" related to church or places of birth or nurture have theological content to inform ecological theology?

5. As leaders, how do we faithfully bear witness to such suffering and evoke the eco-theological imagination of persons in our ministry settings?
    a. How can we shape and form the Word such that we are faithful to what all our writings, indicating that we are not simply responsible to and for creation, but part thereof (oneness, in community with, etc.)?
    b. In what ways can we guard against our own leadership tendencies to overconsume in our efforts to produce?
6. Are we, as humanity, capable of doing no harm?

NOTES

Chapter 1: Greening Death

2 ***the Black Church:*** Like C. Eric Lincoln, Lawrence H. Mamiya, other scholars, and much of the general public, I use "Black Church" as a kind of "sociological and theological shorthand reference to the pluralism of Black Christian churches in the United States." C. Eric Lincoln and Lawrence H. Mamiya, *The Black Church in the African American Experience* (Duke University Press, 1990), 48. Throughout this book, the term "Black Church" refers to an African American collective institution, where "Black church" refers to "congregations" or a particular congregation. Although complex, the Black Church, whether capitalized or not, is one created out of a desire to obtain religious freedom. It is a human community with public and private interests, born from an African traditional religious consciousness, American evangelicalism, and chattel slavery, that was and is necessitated by racism in the church and broader culture for survival and liberation. It affirms the full humanity of all people despite the white supremacist and anti-Black racism that asserts the inherent superiority of white people and inherent inferiority of Black and all other non-white people. The Black Church seeks to encourage and guide its members into a Godly life of salvation, holiness, and covenantal relationship.

Chapter 2: The Setting

15 ***they did not want to consider cremation:*** However, according to Mark Freeman, baby-boomers are preferring a simpler, less expensive funeral, and therefore we have seen the number of cremations rise.

Adam Freeman, "Baby Boomers Transform Funerals" *Wall Street Journal*, December 18, 2002, https://login.proxy.lib.duke.edu/login?url=https://www.proquest.com/docview/398875096?accountid=10598.

17 ***how the Black Church helps the grieving family:*** Sequola Dawson, *The Glad Funeral: An Ongoing Conversation About Funeral Preparation and Process* (Marching Orders Press, 2018).

18 ***grew out of the ugliness of segregation to become mainstays of the Black community:*** Candi Cann, "Black Deaths Matter: Earning the Right to Live—Death and the African-American Funeral Home," *Religions* 11, no. 8 (2020): 390.

18 ***promote excellence in service to the grieving families:*** Funeral Directors and Morticians Association of North Carolina, accessed June 8, 2021, https://www.fdmanc.org/."The National Funeral Directors and Morticians Association (NFDMA) was initially established because the National Funeral Directors' Association (NFDA)—a largely white funeral home association—did not welcome Black funeral home members" (Cann, "Black Deaths Matter," 390).

18 ***the prominent funeral home Scarborough and Hargett of Durham:*** "History and Staff," Scarborough and Hargett, accessed June 8, 2021 https://www.scarboroughhargettcelebration.com/who-we-are/history-and-staff.

19 ***the story of his great-grandfather joining the funeral business:*** Peter McElroy, "The Mortician Who Kept a Neighborhood's History Alive" *Scalawag*, September 29, 2015, https://scalawagmagazine.org/2015/09/mcelroy-skeepie/.

20 ***"Black funeral practices tend to be more old-fashioned":*** McElroy, "The Mortician Who Kept a Neighborhood's History Alive."

20 ***staple of the traditional funeral:*** Natasha Mikles, "Lack of Burial Space is Changing Age-Old Funeral Practices, and in Japan, Tree Burials are Gaining in Popularity," *The Conversation*, accessed June 10, 2021, https://theconversation.com/lack-of-burial-space-is-changing-age-old-funeral-practices-and-in-japan-tree-burials-are-gaining-in-popularity-161323161323?utm_source=newsletter&utm_medium=email&utm_content=premium%2C&utm_campaign=ni_newsletter.

20 ***"many Black funeral homes were themselves owned and operated by preachers":*** Karla Holloway, *Passed On: African American Mourning Stories, A Memorial* (Duke University Press, 2003), 22.

20 ***"we'd just mix our own embalming chemicals":*** Holloway, *Passed On*, 19.

21 ***ways that align with other profit-making businesses in America:*** "Life under empire is always life under threat of assimilation and transformation through the weakening and even loss of cultural identities and religious sensibilities" (Willie James Jennings, *Acts*, Belief, A Theological Commentary on the Bible [Westminster John Knox Press, 2017], 5).

21 ***"Today's Funeral Costs,"*** The North Carolina Funeral Directors Association (NCFDA), accessed June 8, 2021,

https://www.ncfda.org/todays-funeral-costs. However not required for funeralization, it is worth noting that embalming, a major cost to the consumer, was not listed anywhere on the "Today's Funeral Costs" page.

21 ***disposition services:*** Although noted as "could be of different kinds," only two disposition types are listed. Burials and cremations are the traditional two.

22 ***Break-Down of Average Funeral Costs:*** "Today's Funeral Costs," The North Carolina Funeral Directors Association, accessed December 12, 2021, https://www.ncfda.org/todays-funeral-costs.

23 ***"funerals were not lengthy events":*** Virginia R. Beard and William C. Burger, "Change and Innovation in the Funeral Industry: A Typology of Motivations," *OMEGA—Journal of Death and Dying* 75, no. 1 (2017): 47.

23 ***"the increase economic affluence to display wealth":*** Holloway, *Passed On*, 48.

23 ***displays of wealth and classism were in full view:*** Holloway, *Passed On*, 48.

23 ***"a cheap coffin with a lot of paint":*** Holloway, *Passed On*, 32.

23 ***"the negro will do a lot to be sure of a classy funeral":*** Holloway, *Passed On*, 32.

24 ***"cosmological investment in ancestors":*** LaTrese Evette Adkins, "And Who Has the Body? The Historical Significance of African American Funerary Display" (PhD diss., Michigan State University, 2003).

24 ***encourage a view of each life as important:*** McElroy, "The Mortician Who Kept a Neighborhood's History Alive."

25 ***our current systems continue to traumatize Black people:*** Prentis Hemphill, https://prentishemphill.com/, accessed November 14, 2021.

25 ***"I cannot make her beautiful":*** With no ill intent, this mortician has thoughts of "making beautiful" and what constitutes beauty.

26 ***"we are going to do it in style":*** Holloway, *Passed On*, 180.

26 ***"African Americans have always used death material culture to resist":*** Dr. Kami Fletcher, "Y'all see the gold casket right?," Twitter (now X), June 4, 2020, https://twitter.com/kamifletcher36/status/1268580673515851776?s=12&fbclid=IwAR39WW6NS7L_sR5FPLLT1XYP75JJE1SU0FZsRR6ev3Ie70EfM840TCFPBrU.

26 ***expressions or symbols of riches:*** Jeffrey A. Tucker "Why Drug Dealers, Rappers, and Pimps Wear Their Wealth," American Institute of Economic Research, February 14, 2018 https://www.aier.org/article/why-drug-dealers-rappers-and-pimps-wear-their-wealth/. An example of colloquialism or slang might resemble: "having some bling-bling" (meaning I have something that is eye-catchy; something of beauty/worth/value) or "I got my *duckies* (dollars) in a row."

28 ***Westernized funeral industry is not one that nourishes the planet:*** Caitlin Doughty, "A Burial Practice That Nourishes the Planet," TEDMED, November 2016, https://www.ted.com/talks/caitlin_doughty_a_burial_practice_that_nourishes_the_planet.

28 ***"contemporary funeral practices and cemeteries are ecologically problematic":*** Alexandra Harker,

"Landscapes of the Dead: An Argument for Conservation Burial," *Berkeley Planning Journal* 25, no. 1 (2012), http://dx.doi.org/10.5070/BP325111923.

29 ***there is no state law that requires embalming:*** "The FTC Funeral Rule," accessed May 27, 2021, https://www.consumer.ftc.gov/articles/0300-ftc-funeral-rule.

29 ***"funeral homes typically consider embalming the cornerstone of the funeral package":*** Cann, "Black Deaths Matter," 390.

30 ***"the process of removing blood and fluids from the dead body and inserting preservatives":*** "Embalming Definition," Green Burial Council, accessed November 14, 2021, https://www.greenburialcouncil.org/green-burial-glossary.html.

30 ***embalming is not for long-term preservation of the body:*** Lee Webster, *Changing Landscapes: Exploring the Growth of Ethical, Compassionate, and Environmentally Sustainable Green Funeral Practices* (Green Burial Council International, 2017).

30 ***"classify formaldehyde as a hazardous waste":*** "Groundwater Pollution and Radiation Contamination in Cemeteries and Local Communities," *Disabled World Journal*, accessed June 3, 2021, https://www.disabled-world.com/health/cemetery.php.

31 ***"Embalming fluid is a solution used to temporarily preserve a corpse after death":*** Victoria J. Haneman, "Tax Incentives for Green Burial" (February 12, 2020), *Nevada Law Journal* 21, no. 491 (2021), http://dx.doi.org/10.2139/ssrn.3537225.

31 ***"problems were caused by leachate from casket, vault, or embalming fluid":*** Webster, *Changing Landscapes*, 248.

32 ***"African American people believe in funerals":*** Adkins, *And Who Has the Body?*

33 ***cremation has become a common consideration:*** According to National Funeral Directors Association's 2020 Cremation and Burial Report, the projected cremation rate for 2020 was 56% (up 8.1% from 2015).

33 ***green disposal of one's corpse remains a topic rarely discussed:*** Victoria J. Haneman, "Tax Incentives for Green Burial (February 12, 2020)," *Nevada Law Journal*, 491 (2021), https://ssrn.com/abstract=3537225.

34 ***funeral costs are not rising as fast as the rate of inflation:*** National Funeral Director Association (NFDA), "2019 General Price List Study Shows Funeral Costs Not Rising as Fast as Rate of Inflation," accessed May 13, 2021, https://www.nfda.org/news/media-center/nfda-news-releases/id/4797/2019-nfda-general-price-list-study-shows-funeral-costs-not-rising-as-fast-as-rate-of-inflation.

34 ***"paying for funerals with livestock":*** Beverly Bunch-Lyons, "Ours is a Business of Loyalty': African American Funeral Homeowners in Southern Cities," *The Southern Quarterly* 53, no. 1 (2015): 57–71, https://www.muse.jhu.edu/article/605769.

35 ***by 2035, the rate of cremation in all fifty states is expected to exceed 50 percent:*** "Cremation On the Rise: NFDA Predicts the National Cremation Rate Will Climb by a Third Within Twenty Years," National Funeral Directors Association, accessed June 3, 2021, https://nfda.org/news/media-center/nfda-news-releases/id/3526.

35 ***we have seen the number of cremations rise:*** Freeman, "Baby Boomers Transform Funerals."

37 ***driven by interest in profit through the sale of grave materials:*** Holloway, *Passed On*, 44.

38 ***"the task of prophetic ministry":*** Walter Brueggemann, *Prophetic Imagination* (Fortress Press, 2001), 3.

39 ***"a slothfulness in addressing new funeral trends":*** Dawson, *The Glad Funeral*, 18.

40 ***"theoretically, all funerals may be remarkably similar and uniform in appearance":*** Dawson, *The Glad Funeral*, 50.

40 ***"African funerals are always a community affair":*** Schuler, "AIDS Crisis a Boom for Funeral Industry."

41 ***the consequences that follow from these practices:*** It is widely known that the deceased's body has been embalmed by an embalmer—a living breathing person who has been exposed to deadly chemicals. Yet, the Black Church remains silent. "Embalmers are at an 8+ times higher risk of contracting leukemia (*Journal of the National Cancer Institute*, 11.24.09) and a 3 times higher risk of ALS (*Journal of Neurology, Neurosurgery & Psychiatry*, 7.13.15)," Webster, *Changing Landscapes*, 100.

41 ***church funeral processes:*** I speak of this church process more extensively in my book, *The Glad Funeral.*

42 ***"slaves lived closer to the ground":*** Mart A. Stewart, "Slavery and the Origins of African American Environmentalism," in *To Love the Wind and the Rain: African Americans and Environmental History* (University of Pittsburgh Press, 2006).

42 ***"what we are really dealing with is a crisis of culture":*** Norman Wirbza, "Thanks for the Dirt," in *Diversity and Dominion: Dialogues in Ecology, Ethics, and Theology*, ed. Kyle S. van Houtan (Cascade Books, 2010).

42 ***as close to us as our "Westernized" culture allows:*** What does our "Westernized" culture allow? For example, in many cases, slaves were not in control of their own burial practices. "By the late 1700s, African influences in burial practices are considered to have 'faded out' or at least have been fading; since the nineteenth century, most African American burials tended to be in line with European-American and Christian practice (and both were based on traditional European burial practices, such as head to the west, feet to the east). African Americans most often had little control over their own burials during slavery times, and in Chapel Hill burials were likely to have been "controlled" in one way or another by the University and/or Chapel Hill VIP's or society, especially when buried in one of the local public cemeteries such as what is now known as the Old Chapel Hill Cemetery. Certain African American burial practices (with regards to material culture) used in other Southern cemeteries, both urban and rural, do not seem to have been utilized in Chapel Hill or Carrboro, or at least weren't allowed by the municipal authorities to remain and were removed. At best they were extremely limited, as no instances besides "homemade" headstones have been documented in, for instance, the Old Chapel Hill Cemetery. Instances have been documented, however, in rural Orange County cemeteries utilized by people of color, particularly African Americans" (Steve J. Rankin, "A Segregated Part of Heaven: The History of the West Chapel Hill Cemetery," May 2011, https://cemeterycensus.com/nc/orng/075/075-wchcem-report.pdf).

42 ***now leads environmental crisis efforts:*** As a previous member of the Green Burial Council and a continued supporter and advocate of a green community and greening the Church, I have seen that white people in the United States with power and expanded resources have made substantial movement in this area while the Black community still follows. The question is often raised, "How best to incorporate or bring people of color to the table?"

42 ***environmentalism:*** Merriam-Webster defines environmentalism as "advocacy of the preservation, restoration, or improvement of the natural environment."

43 ***my dissertation:*** Sequola Dawson (McNeill), *Telerobotic Operator Risk-Taking Behavior: An Exploratory Investigation in Hazardous Material Handling*, PhD diss, North Carolina Agricultural and Technical State (A&T State) University, 2009.

44 ***risk-taking behavioral theory:*** Dawson (McNeill), *Telerobotic Operator Risk-Taking Behavior.* My background and prior research studies as an engineer involved the effects of remote operators who managed the handling of hazardous material. I concluded that the operators (stewards of skilled mastery) being at a distance and having a greater protection level, exhibited greater risk-taking behavior regarding the hazardous situation than those who operated locally and on site. In other words, the operator's decision-making proved to be riskier (lackadaisical or undisciplined) in any emergency, when the threat did not appear to be proximate. Thus, my research concluded that there is a correlation between distance (whether perceived or actual) and behavior, which affects outcomes and consequences.

Might this distance theory investigation be applied beyond the telerobotic environment in which it was founded? Although distance might not be a slam dunk or a smoking gun relating to home, however, I do think the idea of hazardous materials, hazardous material handling, and risk-taking behavior will come into play in a subsequent chapter involving Black churches, the Black funeral industry, and the impact of toxicity from embalming bodies. This idea may resonate with criticisms from Wendell Berry about our economy: because we are removed from where resources are extracted or food is produced, we are more likely to abuse it and less likely to love it because it is "foreign" to us. Wendell Berry, "The Idea of a Local Economy," *Orion Magazine*, accessed January 1, 2022, https://orionmagazine.org/article/the-idea-of-a-local-economy/.

44 ***"have acted as if they owned the world's resources":*** James Cone, "Whose Earth Is It Anyway?" in *Earth & Word: Classic Sermons on Saving the Planet* (Continuum, 2007), 121.

45 ***"Climate change is now a very familiar phrase":*** Christy Merrick and Rev. Brenda Girton-Mitchell, *African Americans and Climate Change: Adult Education Curriculum* (National Council of Churches USA, 2009), https://www.calameo.com/books/000571242d5049a40aed4.

45 ***"accepted the responsibility to address problems that have a negative impact on our communities":*** Merrick and Girton-Mitchell, *African Americans and Climate Change*.

45 ***"turned its much-needed attention toward ecological issues in the early 1990s":*** Cone, "Whose Earth Is It Anyway?," 117. However, Cone's position is likely not

affirmed by many other scholars. Because the '90s was a time of market growth, neoliberal politics, and some form of the prosperity gospel, it might be difficult to conceive that Black church leaders were focused on the environment and embodying ecological faith in this decade.

45 ***the Black Church has an opportunity to reclaim the goodness of the land:*** Betty Holley, "An Invitation to Pursue the Ecological Conversion," *Christian Recorder*, March 15, 2020.

46 ***Black liberation theology includes the fight for justice for life in all forms:*** Cone, "Whose Earth Is it Anyway?," 120.

46 ***this does not imply that the poor have no agency in the present global crisis:*** Michael Northcott, *A Moral Climate: The Ethics of Global Warming* (Darton, Longman, and Todd, 2010).

46 ***studies have found:*** John M. Ostheimer and Leonard G. Ritt, *Environment, Energy, and Black Americans*. Sage Research Papers in the Social Sciences: Human Ecology Series (Sage, 1976), 90–25. Matthew A. Crenson, *The Un-Politics of Air Pollution: A Study of Non-Decision Making in the Cities* (Johns Hopkins Press, 1971), 15. D. E. LaHart, *The Influence of Knowledge on Young People's Perceptions About Wildlife* (Florida State University, College of Education, 1978). R. H. Giles Jr., "Wildlife Units and Philosophies," Virginia Tech Forester Student Annual (1957): 488–499.

47 ***the Black Church and its community should be held accountable:*** Elder Betty Holley, "Creation in Crisis: What Jesus Offers," *Christian Recorder*, August 16, 2019, https://www.thechristianrecorder.com/articles/creation-in-crisis-what-jesus-offers/.

47 ***"this call to repentance is particularly urgent":*** Sarah Musser, "Comfort in the Whirlwind? Job, Creation, and Environmental Degradation," *Word & World* 32, no. 3 (2012): 286–293.

48 ***"reverence for the earth and reverence for God cannot be separated":*** Ellen Davis, *Getting Involved with God: Rediscovering the Old Testament* (Rowman & Littlefield, 2001), 184.

48 ***"soil is not dirt":*** Fred Bahnson, "Soil and Sacrament: A Spiritual Memoir of Food and Faith," *Faith and Leadership*, August 12, 2013. https://faithandleadership.com/soil-and-sacrament-spiritual-memoir-food-and-faith.

48 ***"race and place are two sides of the same coin":*** Willie Jennings, "The Quadcast: What Does Theology Say About Ecology," Yale Divinity School, 2019, https://soundcloud.com/yaleuniversity/the-quadcast-what-does-theology-say-about-ecology.

48 ***an eco-theological vision of God's creation:*** Jennings, "The Quadcast."

49 ***studies on the environment and the Black community:*** Studies of Black Environmentalism are well documented and show the Black community as being less active in environmental justice than the white community. Although environmental hazards impact the Black community far greater than the white community, it appears that the interest in environmental issues is lesser in the Black community. Stephen Kellert in "Urban American Perceptions of Animals and the Natural Environment" found Black adults to be substantially less interested in, concerned about, and informed about the natural environment than whites. Kellert and Westervelt in "Children's Attitudes, Knowledge, and Behaviors Toward Animals" found nonwhite children to be

less knowledgeable about and less interested in wildlife. More recent research from Cassandra Johnson, J. M. Bowker, John Bergstrom, and H. Ken Cordell in "Wilderness Values in America: Does Immigrant Status or Ethnicity Matter?" compares wilderness values for African Americans, Hispanics, Asians, and whites. It reveals that minority groups were significantly less likely than whites to visit federally designated wilderness areas. Yet, Julia Parker, in "Environmentalism of African Americans: An Analysis of the Subculture and Barriers Theories," challenges many of the early theories suggesting that "it remains unclear whether differences between African Americans and Euro-Americans are manifest in terms of environmentalism." However, Parker notes that barriers to environmental behavior, in the form of feelings of powerlessness, are a factor in understanding environmentalism of African Americans; that African Americans are more incline to participate if it is believed that their actions will make a difference.

50 ***an extensive study on Blacks and the environment:*** Dorceta Taylor, "Blacks and the Environment: Toward an Explanation of the Concern and Action Gap Between Blacks and Whites," *Environment and Behavior* 21, no. 2 (1989): 175–206.

50 ***"an expansion of the civil rights agenda":*** Taylor, "Blacks and the Environment," 200. It is worth noting that the National Association for the Advancement of Colored People (NAACP) Environmental and Climate Justice Program, recognizes environmental and climate justice as civil rights issue. It seeks to meet the challenge of environmental injustice, including the proliferation of climate change that systematically impacts communities

of color and low-income communities in the United States and around the world, by addressing harmful emissions, advancing clean energy, and strengthening resilience and livability in community. The NAACP is a civil rights organization in the United States, formed in 1909 as an interracial endeavor to advance justice for African Americans by a group including W. E. B. Du Bois, Ida B. Wells, Thurgood Marshall, and many other giants of the civil rights movement. https://naacp.org/know-issues/environmental-climate-justice, accessed February 20, 2022.

50 ***"humans are in effect in charge of the climate of the planet":*** Northcott, *A Moral Climate*, 22–29.

51 ***environmental injustice:*** Philip J. Landrigan, Virginia A. Rauh, and Maida P. Galvez, "Environmental Justice and the Health of Children," *The Mount Sinai Journal of Medicine* 77, no. 2 (2010): 178–187, https://doi.org/10.1002/msj.20173.

51 ***"environmental injustice contributes to disparities in health status":*** Landrigan, Rauh, and Galvez, "Environmental Justice and the Health of Children." In addition, Dan Leif reports that "In many communities, waste facilities are situated closer to the homes of minority populations than to the neighborhoods of whites. A 2007 study from the United Church of Christ Justice and Witness Ministries found people of color make up most residents living within 1.8 miles of America's hazardous waste facilities. A 2016 study from University of Michigan researchers looked at over thirty years of data and found a troubling pattern of cities targeting minority neighborhoods when building hazardous waste operations. It is this type of geographic disparity—in

waste and recycling, as well as in other industrial sectors—that has contributed to the fact that minority populations in this country bear the brunt of industrial pollution. Research from the University of Minnesota and the National Science Foundation has found people of color in the United States are on average exposed to 38 percent more nitrogen dioxide than whites (nitrogen dioxide is a widespread air pollutant formed when fossil fuels are burned)" (Dan Leif, "Editor's Opinion: We All Have a Role in Advancing Racial Justice," *Plastics: Recycling Update* (A Resource Recycling, Corporation Publication), accessed March 5, 2021, https://resource-recycling.com/plastics/2020/06/10/editors-opinion-we-all-have-a-role-in-advancing-racial-justice/).

52 ***"People of color are not treated seriously":*** Cone, "Whose Earth Is It Anyway?," 121.

52 ***"how can we create a genuinely mutual ecological dialogue":*** Cone, "Whose Earth Is It Anyway?," 121.

53 ***the woods as sanctuary:*** Cassandra Y. Johnson and Josh McDaniel, "Turpentine Negro," in *To Love the Wind and the Rain: African Americans and Environmental History* (University of Pittsburgh Press, 2006).

53 ***the beauty of planting, flowers, and gardening:*** Dianne D. Glave, "'A Garden So Brilliant with Colors, So Original in its Design:' Rural African American Women, Gardening, Progressive Reform, and the Foundation of an African American Environmental Perspective," *Environmental History* 8, no. 3 (2003), 395.

54 ***"the sacred encompasses the realities of God":*** Kenyatta Gilbert, *Exodus Preaching: Crafting Sermons About Justice and Hope* (Abingdon Press, 2018).

55 ***"holiness is the character of a community":*** Ellen Davis, *Scripture, Culture, and Agriculture: An Agrarian Reading of the Bible* (Cambridge University Press, 2008), 56–57.

55 ***"the Church is one place where our public and private commitments meet":*** Victor Anderson, "The Black Church and the Curious Body of the Black Homosexual," in *Loving the Black Body: Black Religious Studies and the Erotic*, ed. Anthony B. Pinn and Dwight N. Hopkins (Palgrave, 2004), 310.

56 ***"the cultural womb of the Black community":*** C. Eric Lincoln and Lawrence H. Mamiya, *The Black Church in the African American Experience* (Duke University Press, 1990), 8.

56 ***the "soul" as the center of a person's life:*** Christopher A. Beeley, *Leading God's People: Wisdom from the Early Church for Today* (Eerdmans, 2012), 57.

57 ***"our materialistic values will be challenged and transformed":*** Beeley, *Leading God's People.*

57 ***a healthy or a wholesome materiality:*** Davis, *Getting Involved with God: Rediscovering the Old Testament*, 190. Davis suggests that a healthy materiality is the first principle of a biblical ecology.

Chapter 3: Raised Awareness

64 ***"our goal is to change the world we understand":*** Jennings, "The Quadcast."

68 ***"traditional cemeteries put roughly the following into our soil":*** Lee Webster, *Changing Landscapes: Exploring the Growth of Ethical, Compassionate, and*

Environmentally Sustainable Green Funeral Practices (CreateSpace Independent Publishing Platform, 2017), 99–100.

68 ***National Funeral Director Association (NFDA):*** According to their website www.nfda.org, the NFDA is the world's largest association in support of funeral professionals providing the most comprehensive innovative tools and resources for the funeral director.

68 ***annual Cremation and Burial Report:*** *NFDA 2020 Cremation and Burial Report*. National Funeral Directors Association. Brookfield, WI.

68 ***air pollution to be of grave concern:*** Duke Health, "Higher Rates of Alzheimer's Deaths, Hospitalizations Correlate with Air Pollution," https://tinyurl.com/y6ydx6rc.

69 ***Black funeral practices tend to be more old-fashioned:*** Peter McElroy, "The Mortician Who Kept a Neighborhood's History Alive," *Scalawag* (September 29, 2015), accessed June 3, 2021, https://scalawagmagazine.org/2015/09/mcelroy-skeepie/In 1906, John Clarence Scarborough, Sr., (John Clarence Scarborough III's grandfather) the first African American in North Carolina to be a licensed funeral director.

69 ***concern about the environmental impact of conventional burials and cremations mounts:*** Dominique Mosbergen, "Death Has a Climate Change Problem," *HuffPost*, August 31, 2021, https://www.huffpost.com/entry/green-death-care-practices-water-cremation-natural-organic-reduction_n_6116c41fe4b0a2603b7db97a.

69 ***baby boomers are fiercely transforming the industry:*** Adam L. Freeman, "Baby Boomers Transform Funerals," *Wall Street Journal*, December 18, 2002.

70 ***"average funeral with a casket and burial vault costs":*** Freeman, "Baby Boomers Transform Funerals."

70 ***traditional funeral practices with conventional burials and cremations are problematic:*** Mosbergen, "Death Has a Climate Change Problem."

71 ***the ecology of God:*** Ulrich Kortner, "Ecological Ethics and Creation Faith," *HTS: Theological Studies* 72, no. 4 (2016): 2. Kortner discusses Jürgen Moltmann's ecology of God which "is oriented toward the welfare and the salvation of the entire creation." John Hart, *What Are They Saying About Environmental Theology?* (Paulist Press, 2004), 10–11. Hart extends environmentalism toward God. By offering a theology that is concerned with the intrinsic value of all creatures and earth, responsibility of the usage of earth's resources a sense of intergenerational responsibility and a heightened consciousness of the immanence of the Creator in creation.

71 ***an environmental crisis that impacts all:*** "Our extinction is imminent," proclaimed Saint Lucia's Prime Minister, Allen Chastanet as he addressed the UN Conference on Trade and Development after visiting the Bahamas. "No Exit Plan for Small Islands on Climate Crisis Frontlines," UN Trade & Development, September 10, 2019, https://unctad.org/en/pages/newsdetails.aspx?OriginalVersionID=2186.

"The potential risk of multi-breadbasket failure is increasing," argues Cynthia Rosenzweig, a senior NASA scientist and one of the lead authors of the recent UN report on climate change and land. "Climate Change Threatens the World's Food Supply, United Nations Warn," *New York Times*, August 8, 2019, https://www.nytimes.com/2019/08/08/climate/climate-change-food-supply.html.

"Every major oil company is betting heavily against a 1.5-degree Celsius world and investing in projects that are contrary to the Paris goals" according to Carbon Tracker's co-author. Ron Russo, "Big Oil Undermines U.N. Climate Goals with $50 billion of New Projects," *Reuters*, September 9, 2019, https://www.reuters.com/article/us-climate-change-oil/big-oil-undermines-u-n-climate-goals-with-50-billion-of-new-projects-report-idUSKCN1VQ2WC.

Human behavior contributes to climate change. "It has been clear for decades that the Earth's climate is changing, and the role of human influence on the climate system is undisputed," said French scientist Valerie Masson-Delmotte. The article continues to proclaim that "the evidence is clear that carbon dioxide (CO_2) is the main driver of climate change, even as other greenhouse gases and air pollutants also affect the climate." "Climate Change Widespread, Rapid, and Intensifying—IPCC," Intergovernmental Panel on Climate Change (IPCC), August 9, 2019, https://www.ipcc.ch/2021/08/09/ar6-wg1-20210809-pr/.

"Although variability is large, trends associated with human influences are evident in the environment in which hurricanes form, and our physical understanding suggests that the intensity of and rainfalls from hurricanes are probably increasing," even if this increase cannot yet be proven with a formal statistical test argues J. T. Houghton et al. (eds.), in *Climate Change 2001: The Scientific Basis*, published for the Intergovernmental Panel on Climate Change (Cambridge University Press, 2001).

71 ***"the most far-reaching theological crisis ever":*** Ellen Davis, *Getting Involved with God: Rediscovering the Old Testament* (Cowley Publishing, 2001), 183.

71 ***"already affecting many weather and climate extremes":*** "IPCC Report: 'Code Red' for Human Driven Global Heating, Warns UN Chief," *UN News*, August 9, 2021. https://news.un.org/en/story/2021/08/1097362.

71 ***"there is still time to limit climate change":*** "IPCC Report: 'Code Red'."

72 ***keep our global warming temperature below 1.5 degrees Celsius:*** Intergovernmental Panel on Climate Change (IPCC), *Special Report: Global Warming of 1.5°C*, accessed February 28, 2022, https://www.ipcc.ch/sr15/.

72 ***"the clarion call for people all over this earth":*** Betty Holley, "Food Justice: African Americans' Food Sovereignty Movements," *Christian Recorder*, January 18, 2020, https://www.thechristianrecorder.com/articles/food-justice-african-americans-food-sovereignty-movements/.

72 ***"an ongoing call of responsibility":*** Davis, *Getting Involved with God*, 184.

73 ***"embalming the deceased generally means that visitation will be held":*** Cann, "Black Deaths Matter," 390.

73 ***look to Leviticus for revelation:*** Everett Fox, *The Five Books of Moses*, The Schocken Bible, vol. 1 (World Publishing, 1990).

74 ***"the domain of the sacred expands":*** Jacob Milgrom, *Leviticus: A Book of Ritual and Ethics* (Fortress Press, 2004).

75 ***"reverence for the earth and reverence for God cannot be separated":*** Davis, *Getting Involved with God*, 184.

75 ***God's covenantal relationship is with Israel (people), and the land:*** The land includes the plants and the animals, as well (Genesis 9).

75 **adamah *represents fertile soil:*** Ellen Davis, *Opening Israel's Scriptures* (Oxford University Press, 2019), 22. Here, Davis further explains that *soil* is "the substance from which human life is drawn and on which it depends."

77 ***a violation of covenant:*** Ellen Davis, *Scripture, Culture, and Agriculture: An Agrarian Reading of the Bible* (Cambridge University Press, 2008), 17.

78 ***"a theologically profound vision":*** Davis, *Scripture, Culture, and Agriculture*, 83.

78 ***a widespread Christian disregard for Leviticus:*** Davis, *Opening Israel's Scriptures*, 62.

78 ***"profound connection between humans and land":*** Davis, *Opening Israel's Scriptures*, 77.

79 ***"Land was the means of subsistence for nearly every Israelite":*** Davis, *Opening Israel's Scriptures.*

79 ***Aaron, Israel's first high priest:*** Ellen Davis, *Preaching the Luminous Word: Biblical Sermons and Homiletical Essays* (Eerdmans, 2016), 35.

79 ***"Israel should live out its Sinai-based vocation":*** Davis, *Opening Israel's Scriptures*, 72.

80 ***we practice rituals and hold them sacred:*** Karla Holloway, *Passed On: African American Mourning Stories, A Memorial* (Duke University Press, 2003), 151.

80 ***from righteousness comes justice:*** Israel Knohl, *The Sanctuary of Silence: The Priestly Torah and the Holiness School* (Eisenbrauns, 2007).

80 ***the land has a moral sensitivity:*** Davis, *Scripture, Culture, and Agriculture*, 110.

80 ***"the land cares how we use or misuse it":*** Davis, *Scripture, Culture, and Agriculture.*

80 ***"sensitivity that perceives land a living being":*** Davis, *Scripture, Culture, and Agriculture.*

81 ***God is calling us to it:*** Davis, *Getting Involved with God*, 183; Norman Wirzba, "Thanks for the Dirt: Gratitude as the Basis for Environmental Ethics," in *Diversity and Dominion: Dialogues in Ecology, Ethics, and Theology*, ed. Kyle S. Van Houten and Michael Northcott (Wipf & Stock, 2010), 79.

81 ***"land is an active participant in covenantal living":*** Davis, *Opening Israel's Scriptures*, 72.

82 ***agrarian reading of Leviticus:*** Davis, *Scripture, Culture, and Agriculture*, 80.

82 ***seeing with God and with God's original intent:*** Davis, *Scripture, Culture, and Agriculture.* According to Davis, this concept is based on Abraham Heschel's study of the Prophets.

82 ***a polluted temple:*** Milgrom, *Leviticus*, 9, 32.

83 ***"so that heaven may be more beautiful":*** Davis, *Preaching the Luminous Word*, 37.

83 ***"robbed of the courage and power to think":*** Walter Brueggemann, *The Prophetic Imagination* (Fortress Press, 2001), 39.

83 ***it is time to reconsider the doctrine of creation:*** Colin Gunton, *The Doctrine of Creation: Essays in Dogmatics, History, and Philosophy* (T&T Clark, 1997), 2, 5. Gunton says that the doctrine of creation is different from that of Christology. Christology is concerned with God's involvement in the world "already" made, but creation has to do with the constituting of that world. Gunton suggests moving beyond the "largely" ecological to include other dimensions, specifically, the aesthetics/art.

Gunton says that art involves one of the many *human ways* of relating to the material world. Gunton further asserts that "so anxious have theologians been to demonstrate the credibility of the doctrine of creation by using the natural world to provide evidence of its truth, that the reverse relation [using truth, aesthetics and art of the material world, to provide evidence of the natural world] has been neglected."

83 ***one must have a deep sense of connectivity:*** Jennings, "The Quadcast: What Does Theology Say About Ecology?" From Augustine, *Conf.* 12.7. to Karl Barth, *Church Dogmatics* (1969) to the present, the church and Christians continue to speak regarding creation. The goal here is to aid in the framing of creation around God's original intent of closeness without the separation of Creator and creation and the relationship that exists not only between but also inside of the two.

83 ***"exploration of the relationship between God and humanity":*** Davis, *Scripture, Culture, and Agriculture*, 8.

84 ***Soil is a complex web of relationships:*** Wirzba, "Thanks for the Dirt," 79.

85 ***an expectation of covenantal loyalty:*** Lack of loyalty with humanity's lawlessness and violence (Genesis 6—dominion gone wrong) leads to God's destruction of the earth, which God then makes allowances for in Genesis 9.

85 ***"skilled mastery that represents God and God's interest":*** Davis, *Opening Israel's Scriptures*, 8–13.

86 ***"clothe thyself in beauty":*** Philip Schaff, *Nicene and Post-Nicene Fathers*, Series II, vol. 10 (Christian Classics Ethereal Library, 2013). [Baruch 5:1]. [Ambrose of Milan, Book I.IX.812.], accessed June 20, 2020, https://www.ccel.org.

86 ***"the beauty of the perishable body":*** Schaff, *Nicene and Post-Nicene Fathers*, 812.

86 ***"the comeliness of virtue":*** Schaff, *Nicene and Post-Nicene Fathers*, Chapter VI, 805.

87 ***the Church has largely been silent on climate change:*** Betty Holley, "Educating for Sustainability," *Christian Recorder*, June 11, 2017.

87 ***wisdom is to know the good:*** Plato, *The Republic*, accessed November 21, 2021,https://classics.mit.edu/Plato/republic.mb.txt; William Harmless, *Augustine in His Own Words* (Catholic University of America Press, 2010).

87 ***there is no separation of wisdom and justice:*** Schaff, *Nicene and Post-Nicene Fathers*, Chapter IX, 140.

88 ***the integrity of the life of the inner person:*** Schaff, *Nicene and Post-Nicene Fathers*, Introduction, 28.

89 ***"we are possessed by (belong to God)":*** Jennings, "The Quadcast: What Does Theology Say About Ecology?"

89 ***"1 Peter 2:9":*** This is a very familiar scripture in the Black Church and is often read from the King James Version (KJV).

90 ***New Interpreter's Bible points us to Colossians:*** The New Interpreter's Bible, Ministry Matters, Duke Library, accessed January 7, 2022.

90 ***Colossians 1:12–14:*** Other ancient authorities interpret *who has enabled you* as *who has called you.*

91 ***"We have tilled the adamah but have not kept it":*** Fred Bahnson, *Soil and Sacrament: A Spiritual Memoir of Food and Faith*, excerpt on Faith and Leadership, August 12, 2013. https://faithandleadership.com/soil-and-sacrament-spiritual-memoir-food-and-faith.

91 ***"life that is healthful":*** Davis, *Scripture, Culture, and Agriculture*, 56.

91 ***"a single harmonious order":*** Davis, *Scripture, Culture, and Agriculture*, 57.

92 ***ecological faith:*** At the time of publishing, the direct origin of the term *ecological faith* could not be gathered. However, I use the term *ecological faith* in association with an active display of the embodiment of an ecology theology.

92 ***when death occurs, the church is often silent about its (covenantal) responsibility to the environment:*** In general, churches need to be more concerned about the environment across all aspects of its ministry, not just in how it approaches death.

92 ***a glad funeral:*** See my book *The Glad Funeral: An Ongoing Conversation About Funeral Preparation and Process* (Marching Orders Press, 2018).

Chapter 4: The Green Funeral

94 ***green burial is about a return to the past:*** Suzanne Kelly, *Greening Death: Reclaiming Burial Practices and Restoring Our Tie to the Earth* (Rowman & Littlefield, 2015), 4.

94 ***natural burial principles and practices:*** Marshall Trimble, "Native American Burial Customs," *True West*, January 25, 2020. https://truewestmagazine.com/native-american-burial-customs/. Richard Twiss, *Rescuing the Gospel from the Cowboys: A Native American Expression of the Jesus Way* (InterVarsity Press, 2015). Ian Barnes, *The Historical Atlas of Native Americans* (Chartwell Books, 2009).

94 ***the first green or natural, burial ground:*** Suzanne Kelly, *Greening Death*, 3. Hannah Palko, "Implementing

Aldo Leopold's Ideas Through the Socio-Ecological Practice of Green Burial: Ramsey Creek Preserve in South Carolina, USA," *Socio-Ecological Practice Research* 3 (2021), 441–450. https://doi.org/10.1007/s42532-021-00098-z. Harker, "Landscapes of the Dead."

94 ***three top defining characteristics of any green burial:*** Lee Webster, *Changing Landscapes: Exploring the growth of Ethical, Compassionate, and Environmentally Sustainable Green Funeral Practices* (CreateSpace Independent Publishing Platform, 2017), 102.

95 ***top reasons why people choose to green death:*** Kelly, *Greening Death*. These very reasons may also tend to be problematic or receive pushback.

97 ***environmental activists Rachel Carson and Aldo Leopold:*** See Rachel Carson, *Silent Spring* (1962) and Aldo Leopold, *A Sand County Almanac* (1949).

97 ***2010 New York Times article:*** Quoted in Kelly, *Greening Death*, 126.

98 ***concern regarding burials and soil contamination:*** Cornela Jonker, "Mineral Contamination from Cemetery Soils: Case Study of Zandfontein Cemetery, South Africa," *International Journal of Environmental Research and Public Health* 9, no. 2 (2012).

98 ***"standard bearer of green burial terrain":*** Kelly, *Greening Death*, 86.

98 ***"use of non-toxic and biodegradable materials":*** The Green Burial Council, accessed August 28, 2020, http://greenburialcouncil.org.

98 ***"advocates for green services and products":*** Green Burial Council, http://greenburialcouncil.org.

99 ***a few elements or considerations to help the Black Church rethink funerals:*** Green Burial Council, http://greenburialcouncil.org.

99 ***formaldehyde has been shown to cause health issues for the embalmer:*** Michael Hauptmann et al., "Mortality from Lymphohematopoietic Malignancies and Brain Cancer Among Embalmers Exposed to Formaldehyde," *Journal of the National Cancer Institute* 101, no. 24 (December 16, 2009), 1696–1708.

101 ***conservation certification:*** "Our Standards," Green Burial Council, accessed November 1, 2021, https://www.greenburialcouncil.org/our_standards.html.

101 ***sky burial as seen in the Tibetan culture:*** Claire Elise Thompson, "From Fiction to Reality: Could Forests Replace Cemeteries? From Tree Pods and Mushroom Suits to Pail Old Dirt, Death May Have a Greener Future," *Grist*, September 14, 2021, https://grist.org/fix/green-burial-forest-cemeteries/.

101 ***direct burial:*** The Green Burial Council, Accessed August 28, 2020. http://greenburialcouncil.org.

102 ***Bluestem Cemetery:*** Bluestem is a conservation cemetery founded in Durham County, North Carolina and located in Orange County, North Carolina.

102 ***number of cremations in the United States is rising:*** According to the NFDA's 2021 Cremation and Burial Report, by 2040, the US cremation rate is projected to reach 78.4 percent and burial rate 16 percent.

102 ***not drawn out:*** However, the NFDA reports that 28 percent of Americans claim to have a stronger personal faith since the COVID-19 pandemic. In 2020 and 2021, there was an increase in the number of Americans who feel that religion is a very important component in a funeral according to the NFDA's 2021 Cremation and Burial Report, July 2021.

103 ***option to [formally] view their loved one:*** "Providing All Options: Embalming and Cremation," Cremation Association of North America (CANA), November 3, 2021, https://www.cremationassociation.org/blog/providing-all-options-embalming-and-cremation.

103 ***human composting (recomposing):*** Human Composting: "Other Disposition Options," Green Burial Council, accessed October 19, 2021, https://www.greenburialcouncil.org/other_disposition_options.html; Recompose, accessed October 19, 2021, https://recompose.life/.

103 ***human aquamation (resomation):*** E. Keijzer, "Environmental Impact of Different Funeral Technologies," TNO Report, August 8, 2011, https://www.petmemorialcenter.ca/aquamation/TNO_report_Environmental_impact_of_different_funeral_technologies.pdf.

103 ***aquamation:*** Victoria Haneman, "Tax Incentives for Green Burial," *Nevada Law Journal*, February 12, 2020, https://ssrn.com/abstract=3537225.

104 ***local aquamation charge starts at $1,995:*** Clay-Barnette Funeral Home and Aquamation Center, https://www.claybarnette.com, accessed October 19, 2021; and "Alkaline Hydrolysis," accessed October 19, 2021, https://www.greenburialcouncil.org/other_disposition_options.html. In Danville, Indiana, Bio-Response Solutions acknowledges that "the cost of [aquamation] services and what is included in the price varies greatly by area and provider. Aquamation is comparable in price to flame cremation. It is significantly less costly than burial." Accessed January 7, 2022, https://aquamationinfo.com/faq/.

105 ***new deathcare trends:*** "Other Disposition Options," Green Burial Council, accessed October 19, 2021, https://www.greenburialcouncil.org/other_disposition_options.html. Diversification in the management of the deceased's body and other methods for greening death are known yet may not currently be officially promoted by the GBC. Other diverse methodologies are: promession or cryogenic freezing, the mushroom suit, and capsula mundi.

105 ***Hart offers an environmental theology:*** John Hart, *What Are They Saying About Environmental Theology?* (Paulist Press, 2004), 10–11.

105 ***"our ethical responsibility for the non-human world":*** Douglas Moo, *Creation Care: A Biblical Theology of the Natural World* (Zondervan Academic, 2018), 24.

106 ***the stewardship of God's creation:*** "Creation Care," Lausanne Movement, accessed December 28, 2021, https://lausanne.org/networks/issues/creation-care.

106 ***BioExplorer.net's history of ecology:*** "History of Ecology," Bio Explorer, accessed December 27, 2021, https://www.bioexplorer.net/history_of_biology/ecology/.

107 ***Green The Church:*** "Our Values," Green The Church, accessed December 23, 2021 https://www.greenthechurch.org/our-mission-v2.

107 ***care of the land is intimately tied to Black liberation:*** Yonat Shimron, "Otis Moss III: Care for the Land is Intimately Tied to Black Liberation," *Faith and Leadership*, accessed June 9, 2021, https://faithandleadership.com/otis-moss-iii-care-the-land-intimately-tied-black-liberation. Dianne, D. Glave, "Black Environmental Liberation Theology," in *To Love the Wind and the Rain: African Americans and Environmental History* (University of Pittsburgh Press, 2006).

108 ***"fragile beauty of the fertile earth":*** Davis, *Getting Involved with God*, 184.

108 ***through our abuse of creation:*** Davis, *Scripture, Culture, and Agriculture*, 19. Isaiah 24:5: "The earth also is defiled under the inhabitants thereof; because they have transgressed the laws, changed the ordinance, broken the everlasting covenant."

Chapter 5: To Be a Mango Tree

123 ***the Final Walk:*** The Final Walk (sometimes called a march or The Last Mile) represents a slow, very distinguished step-by-step gait, symbolized by high or exaggerated leg or foot movements as the "stepper" holds on to the casket behind them while it is pushed forward. The original Final Walk was developed to show dignity and respect for the deceased. The Final Walk is orchestrated by or with the assistance of the funeral home usually at the end of the church services and may be conducted with or without music.

To some, the Final Walk is merely a show. In a comment on "The Final Walk" (https://www.youtube.com/watch?v=X3cRbwXPvUw) a person posts, "them darkies really like to put on a show. . ." This racist comment is indicative of the Black funeral being seen as more dramatic than others, as stated earlier. Some have called this walk "tacky," while others can appreciate the thought and the effort behind the Final Walk.

Recently, I witnessed the Final Walk for the first time at the homegoing services for my aunt. Once initiated, I did not know what was happening. The first thing I noticed was that the casket was turned feet-first. Generally, caskets are rolled in a "headfirst" position (this posturing could have been a mistake on the part of the morticians. This infuses or kindles a position of a rush to perform). Secondly, I witnessed the mortician standing at the front of the casket closest to the rear of the church as if he was preparing for embodying or channeling a spirit of movement. Then the mortician thrust his coattail to his rear, which for a quick second draped the casket as it fell. The mortician then took an abnormal stance, stooping downward, and proceeded to walk forward with exaggerated leg and foot movements as the casket was pushed by another member of the funeral home staff out of the church.

After further reflection, this walk was like a living exaggerated cartoon character symbolizing the mourning and the pain of the hour. However, if not carefully done, the Final Walk can be a show or a put on, just like any other act in a play or drama.

The church houses and displays sacred and spirit-filled practices like the reading or the praying of the scriptures, singing, and dancing. Is this Final Walk sacred? Is it sanctioned or deemed lawful by the church? What does the church have to say about this Final Walk? Did the family of the deceased or the church agree to this performance? In my scenario, my family, including my cousins (the children of my dearly beloved aunt) were unaware and were never informed of a Final Walk.

The comment from the website was followed by a comment that appeared to have been posted by a representative of the funeral home and the stepper inside of the video:

> *Hey all thanks for the comments whether they are good or bad but what I will say is at least I*

> *got yawl talking, and besides that, I will also say this. I am the busiest African American–owned funeral home out of the seven here in Rochester, NY, so no matter what you say I am living fine, and people support us. The walk is basically a slow step-by-step walk instead of just pulling the casket out. Giving the person a dignified walk out even if the person wasn't deemed important in life, the morticians give a "worth march" out the church, Texas and Louisiana do it all the time.*

Chapter 7: Staying Woke in Death

157 ***include the care or corruption of creation:*** Dean David E. Goatley, Goodson Chapel Service, November 16, 2021, https://www.youtube.com/watch?v=wz6L4rcWxa0.

157 ***a way of seeing that is bifocal:*** Davis, *Scripture, Culture, and Agriculture*, 14.

158 ***faithfully follow the will of God:*** Dean David E. Goatley, Duke Divinity School Advent Brochure, 2020.

158 ***"pushing-off from our tiptoes":*** Dean Gregory Jones, Duke Divinity School Advent Brochure, 2020.

159 ***"people are waking up to a deeper yearning":*** Kelly, *Greening Death*, 69.

159 ***"theology should not put us to sleep":*** James Cone, "Black Theology and Black Power," lecture, Yale Divinity School, 2017, accessed September 12, 2017, https://www.youtube.com/watch?v=kyP7BrmII9U.

159 ***"always be opened and oriented toward freedom":*** Herbert Robinson Marbury, *Pillars of Cloud and Fire: The Politics of Exodus in African American Biblical Interpretation* (New York University Press, 2015), 6–7, back cover.

Chapter 8: Beauty and Honoring Covenantal Relationships

166 ***"to purse an ecological conversion":*** Dr. Betty Holley, "An Invitation to Pursue the Ecological Conversion," *Christian Recorder*, March 15, 2020.

169 ***the character of holiness and art:*** Brian Horne, "Divine and Human Creativity," in *The Doctrine of Creation: Essays in Dogmatics, History, and Philosophy* (T&T Clark, 2004); Sergei Bulgakov, "Religion and Art," in *The Church of God: An Anglo-Russian Symposium*, ed. E. L. Mascall (SPCK, 1934), 175.